MAKING THE TEAM

Inside the World of Sport Initiations and Hazing

Edited by Jay Johnson and Margery Holman

Canadian Scholars' Press Inc.
Toronto

Making the Team: Inside the World of Sport Initiations and Hazing
edited by Jay Johnson and Margery Holman

First published in 2004 by
Canadian Scholars' Press Inc.
180 Bloor Street West, Suite 801
Toronto, Ontario
M5S 2V6

www.cspi.org

Canadian Scholars' Press gratefully acknowledges financial support for our publishing activities from the Government of Canada through the Book Publishing Industry Development Program (BPIDP) and the Government of Ontario through the Ontario Book Publishing Tax Credit Program.

Library and Archives Canada Cataloguing in Publication

Making the team : inside the world of sport initiations and hazing / edited by Jay Johnson and Margery Holman.

Includes bibliographical references.
ISBN 1-55130-247-0

1. Initiations (into trades, societies, etc.) 2. Hazing. 3. Sports—Sociological aspects.
4. Sports—Social aspects. I. Johnson, Jay II. Holman, Margery Jean

GV706.8.M345 2004   306.4'83   C2004-903726-9

Cover and text design by Hothouse Canada
06   07   08   5   4   3   2

Printed and bound in Canada by AGMV Marquis Imprimeur Inc.

ONTARIO ARTS COUNCIL
CONSEIL DES ARTS DE L'ONTARIO

Table of Contents

Preface

On May 8, 2003, *The Windsor star* reported, as did other media, that "a touch football game between suburban Chicago high school girls turned into a brutal hazing in which players were slapped, punched, doused with paint and splattered in the face with mud and feces." Hazing continues to catch the attention of media and occupy the time of school administrators. It also continues to be a form of indoctrinating neophytes into group-think, earning them the desired team acceptance. Sport organizations often believe that they have hazing under control until a violent or offensive event occurs. This Chicago news item resulted in injury. As well, some participants face criminal charges.

More recently, in September 2003, media reports described a hazing ritual alleged to have taken place during high school football training camp in Pennsylvania. One newspaper reported that three junior varsity players were allegedly sodomized with a broomstick, pine cones, and golf balls while other players watched. This case is currently under investigation.

The trend to set policy against hazing and to speak out against it has been set in the past few years. Administrators have recognized that there are social and legal implications associated with hazing that can be destructive to the athletic experience of many. However, from the recent cases cited here, it is evident that more needs to be done to understand hazing behaviours and to educate about, as well as to regulate, the incorporation of new recruits into the team setting.

This monograph is intended for use by university, college, and high school students, as well as individuals involved in sport leadership as board members, administrators, teachers/coaches, players/athletes, and even team owners. While much of the research and writing about hazing has taken place in university sport, there is much to be learned about the topic from the various chapters of this text for both educational and club sport contexts. The principles remain the same and the moral and legal obligations apply universally.

The book consists of a series of chapters, which can be read independently or consecutively. Of necessity, there is some redundancy; however, the points reiterated are those that should be internalized by anyone involved in sport. The range of authors includes university professors, established authors, current and former athletes, coaches and administrators who possess expertise in sport, a journalist, and graduate students who have studied extensively in the social development of sport.

This book, *Making the team: Inside the world of sport initiations and hazing*, is the first to be published entirely dedicated to the topic of hazing and initiation in athletics. The current text offers material that reflects the challenges faced by those within athletics who want to see hazing practices eliminated, as well as by those who want to see the traditions maintained but evolved into a memorable experience that has positive outcomes for all.

The trend towards transforming athletics into a more humane and democratic environment has met with some resistance. Yet laws, policy, and common sense have driven changes to this end. While hazing events were invisible in the past, some of today's journalists have been more willing to expose the secrets of team hazing traditions. Without knowledge of the behaviours that represent hazing, there is little likelihood that positive change will occur. We hope that by reviewing the chapters in this book, the reader will develop a new perspective on the topic of hazing. The intent is to generate discussion at a level that is normally avoided and to have athletes, coaches, and administrators work together to develop alternative strategies to many of the traditional hazing practices. The text is designed for educators and practitioners. Parts can be read as a novel in a passive way, while others are designed to stimulate debate. Reference is made to numerous Canadian and American cases in the text so that the reader can understand the types of activities that represent hazing and the outcome of hazing practices in the sport culture. These cases provide only a small part of the picture.

Brian Trota and Jay Johnson start us off with an introductory history of the roots of hazing. It provides the reader with an understanding of the original intents of hazing and how these have transferred to the athletic setting with specific purposes. This introduction is followed by Chapter 1, written by sports journalist Laura Robinson. Robinson has been actively researching the traditions and abuses in sport for several years now, sharing her findings in several of her own books. In this chapter, she provides us with real-life stories of hazing practices that have been hurtful to many, yet have been defended by others. She demonstrates how the stories that she shares contribute to the maintenance of a sport culture that is abusive, discriminating, and male-centred. In reading Robinson's chapter, you are likely to experience an array of emotions. Her writings provide the perfect backdrop to approaching the remaining chapters with an open and critical view. Chapter 2, written by Brian Crow and Dennis Phillips, provides an overview of the law. While most of the chapter deals with American law, this is to be expected since various states in the USA have taken the lead in declaring hazing practices illegal. Typically, sports-related litigation in the USA becomes prominent in Canadian sport organizations a short time later. However, because our legal systems are quite different, the chapter contains a section addressing the unique approach through which litigation could proceed in Canada should a case warrant legal action. This is an important chapter for those who might want to know how the law protects their rights, and for those potentially at risk as a respondent to a lawsuit.

In Chapter 3, Greg Malszecki, who has done extensive research concerning military hazing practices, informs the reader of the military roots of hazing. Only in recent years has the public been privy to the hazing practices that new military recruits have been forced to endure. This chapter will give people in sport—leaders, participants, parents, media and fans—a better perspective of the concept of hazing.

The next four chapters provide a theoretical analysis for the understanding of hazing practices in athletics. In Chapter 4, "A Search for a Theoretical Understanding of Hazing Practices in Athletics," Margery Holman provides some insight into the theoretical bases for preserving hazing practices. The chapter illuminates the connections between hierarchy, power, and violence, and also draws gender into the debate. Allan and DeAngelis continue the theoretical discourse in Chapter 5, building upon the concept of power, identifying the role of masculinity, and introducing the potential for change through education. In Chapter 6, Helen Lenskyj focuses on the sexual violence perpetrated through hazing practices. This chapter draws attention to the sexually abusive nature of many hazing activities and to the need for stronger intervention strategies and a transformation of the traditional male sport subcultures. Chapter 7 reports on the results of a study that examined coach perceptions on hazing based upon gender. While female and male coaches did not differ significantly in their views of hazing and its role in sport, the chapter provides some interesting insights by relating the findings to an extensive review of the literature.

Chapter 8 moves away from theory and provides a unique look at the ways in which sportswriters can contribute to the culture that supports hazing. Author Hank Nuwer is one of North America's top researchers and writers on hazing practices, particularly in fraternities. His expertise is shared within this publication. Since media outlets serve a major educating tool for public views, this analysis is critical to the process of change.

The final two chapters, by Jay Johnson with Peter Donnelly and Patricia Miller respectively, provide important strategies in the elimination and/or management of initiation and hazing practices. They look at policy development as a first step for the communication of organizational values and principles. And they go beyond the boardroom approach of policy to the on-sight implementation of an action plan. Alternatives are offered to traditional hazing rituals, alternatives that can accomplish the goal of team-building commonly seen as a critical objective of initiation. These chapters confirm the possibility of positive change that respects traditions, and that contributes to a pleasurable sport experience for all involved.

The editors would like to thank all of the authors who took time from their busy schedules to research and write their chapters. Each one has contributed to a relatively new body of literature that can directly benefit academic institutions and their student bodies in the classroom and in their athletic programs, professional and amateur sport organizations, and community sport programs. Indirectly, the media can develop a deeper understanding of stories on which they report, and the general public can learn more about the hidden practices that are often associated with sport. It is also a must-read for parents, who can prepare their children to deal with hazing by discussing some of these chapters with them, and by helping them develop strategies to challenge inappropriate demands being made of them. Overall, there are few people, particularly among those who have an interest in sporting practices, who will not benefit from at least some of the material presented by our authors.

A Brief History of Hazing

Brian Trota and Jay Johnson

Hazing is by definition a rite of passage wherein youths, neophytes, or rookies are taken through traditional practices by more senior members in order to initiate them into the next stage of their cultural, religious, academic, or athletic lives. Often, however, the hazing ritual serves also to forge and perpetuate a hierarchical and patriarchal structure. While it is difficult to know how long hazing has been with us, similar rites of passages have been part of our society for a long time. Perhaps being aware of hazing's long roots can bring a greater understanding of just how embedded hazing rituals continue to be in our modern-day cultures and traditions. Even in the way we act and think, we might see how we are bound by hierarchical hazing processes.

In many cultures and societies in the world, the origins of hazing rituals span generations, and sometimes centuries. Over time, hazing rituals present common traits. They generally involve one dominant party, whose membership includes the veterans, and one weaker, less-seasoned party, whose members include those not yet officially accepted as group members.

Historically, tradition in the hazing ritual is important to bring a sense of cultural identity to the youth. As noted by Bryshun (1997), in ceremonies conducted by the Zuni tribes of New Mexico and the Nandi tribe of East Africa, boys are transformed into men. Their identities are moulded into one that suits the subculture (Donnelly and Young, 1988). In the Nandi tribe in the early 1800s, a boy was circumcised as part of his transformation into manhood (Toohey and Swann, 1985). The endurance of pain and display of courage in the face of danger are key points in this initiation rite, and serve to separate the men from the boys, and the men from the women (Bryshun, 1997).

EDUCATION AND THE MEDIEVAL UNIVERSITY

The transition to a new phase of life is often celebrated, yet entry into a world of veteran territory is a novel experience. In education, advancing to a university culture represents one of these transitions; thus the beginnings of hazing in the medieval university.

With the rise of "stadium genrales" (precursors to early universities) in Western Europe in the twelfth century, hazing and hazing traditions became an integral part of both academic and social life. At this time, universities were an exclusively male privilege. By the thirteenth century, the word "university" was used for these institutions of higher learning, especially those situated in Paris, Palermo, and Oxford. Hazing rituals and initiating practices were created primarily in order to weed out those who didn't have the physical and mental capacity to reach the status of professor.

THE RISE OF FRATERNITIES IN EIGHTEENTH CENTURY AMERICA

Hazing or "fagging" began in America's educational institutions around 1657. Early fraternities, it appears, were created in order to bring together young men with the same educational background and to provide them with a comfortable environment. Harvard and Yale became perfect settings for the creation and development of these fraternities. Although the original fraternity was the Phi Beta Kappa, created in 1776, many fraternities began to appear in the 1870s all across America.

The actual term "hazing" was not used until after the American Civil War, but the first notable incident of hazing happened in 1657 when two first-year students won a settlement after being hazed (Nuwer, 1990). The first Harvard student to be punished for his participation in hazing practices was Joseph Webb in 1684. He demanded that first-year students attend to him, using force to ensure compliance—in short, he hit them (Nuwer, 1990).

Later, in the eighteenth century, it became the norm for many first-year

Harvard students to become the servants of their older classmates, as it did at Yale and at Williams College, both well into the late nineteenth century. In the latter instance, hazing was used to reinforce subordination, compliance and deference to those more senior (Nuwer, 1990).

In 1873, the first known death related to hazing occurred at Cornell University in New York when a pledge was blindfolded and marched into the countryside by Kappa Alpha members. The members then took off the blindfold and told the pledge to return to the campus, alone. Unaware of his surroundings, the pledge died as a result of a fall. Tragically, another death occurred as a result of a similar hazing practice in 1899 (Nuwer, 1990).

HAZING AT THE UNIVERSITY LEVEL IN THE TWENTIETH CENTURY

After the Second World War, there was a rise of fraternities on college campuses and a corresponding sharp increase in hazing. At Texas A & M, for example, the Dean noted that as a result of the rise of hazing, by 1947, 48% of dormitory students dropped out after the first semester (Bryshun, 1997; Nuwer, 1990).

One of the most publicized university hazing incidents was the death of Chuck Stenzel in 1978 at Alfred University, which occurred while he was being initiated into the Klan Alpine Fraternity. Mr. Stenzel and two other pledges were forcibly locked in the truck of a car and told to drink a pint of bourbon, a bottle of wine and a six-pack of beer. After the pledges had consumed the alcohol, they were left to fight cold temperatures in the trunk of the car for forty minutes. The initiation rite was designed to make them sick so they would vomit. Afterward, the pledges were brought back inside to sleep off their drunkenness. At this point, one of the pledges suffered cardiac arrest, another fell into alcoholic coma, and Mr. Stenzel died of alcohol poisoning (Bryshun, 1997; Hornbuckle, 1988; Nuwer, 1990).

A similarly tragic event occurred on September 23, 2000, when a seventeen-year-old athlete for the rugby team at the University of New Brunswick almost died because of alcohol poisoning at a "rookie party." The team was promptly suspended between September 26 and October 2, 2000. And yet, on October 14 of the same year, in the same province, the Mount St. Allison women's volleyball team was charged in connection with an initiation party which saw rookies "suck beer from condoms, peeing in stolen garbage buckets and nose-writing in cat food casserole" (MacIntyre, 2001).

In the United States, there have also been documented incidents involving violence, including branding. Many black fraternities have been known, for example, to brand their pledges with the Greek letter associated with the respective fraternity. At Ball State University in Missouri in 1987, a student went on record and described the experience of being branded: "Three seconds more—I wouldn't have gotten it ... I was losing my nerve ... The pain isn't intense. You just smell your skin burning and you hear it crackling. To some, that might be enough to drive them crazy. You can't move because they'll make a mistake. Once you move it's hard to correct the mistake" (Nuwer, 1990: 210).

It should be noted that many of these incidents occur during orientation week or "Frosh Week," when first-year students are initiated. During one opening week at the University of Saskatchewan campus, one man was found dead at the bottom of an elevator shaft. There was little doubt about the circumstances of his death since his body was found covered in whipped cream and fire extinguisher fluid (Nuwer, 1990: 250).

Unfortunately, being covered with food and liquids does not appear to be uncommon in hazing rituals. During a similar, though far less deadly, Frosh Week at Queen's University in Kingston, Ontario, first-year engineering students were told to climb a greasy pole, below which was a moat filled with raw sewage and animal parts. The first-year students' task was to capture a sacred tam-o-shanter at the top, while the audience chucked vegetables at them (*Macleans*, January 30, 1995: 18).

HAZING IN THE HIGH-SCHOOL SETTING

Disturbingly, in an Alfred University study (1999), 48% of students who belonged to groups reported being hazed back in high school. Hazing rituals at the high-school level may set up and perpetuate the notion in students and athletes that hazing is something very natural, that it is part of joining any group. This mentality surely breeds a cycle. When hazing begins for an individual in high school, or even in childhood, it may be more readily accepted when the individual continues into college and university years. The individual is not necessarily blind in this acceptance, but may come to believe unconsciously that hazing is part of joining any team or group, that it is an important part of bonding. This kind of belief can be dangerous, given that violent, demeaning, or sexualized behaviour may be an integral part of the so-called bonding tradition.

Nuwer (1990) is an excellent resource for learning about hazing behaviours. For example:

- An early case of hazing in high school happened in 1905 when a thirteen-year-old boy died of pneumonia after being hazed by his peers who stuffed snow into his clothing.
- In 1924, two girls from Brooklyn, New York, had Greek letters branded into their foreheads with nitrate of silver. Sadly, the principal's only response was to say that the sorority that the girls were trying to join had no affiliation with the high school.
- A Loris High School initiate of the National Future Farmers of America had to crawl under an electrified cattle fence while wet and naked. In another case at the same school, initiates were forced to stick bananas up their noses until they bled.

If 24% of varsity athletes surveyed reported being hazed in some fashion at the high-school level, then the examples presented must be less exceptional than they first appear. This percentage represents a significant number, and its implication demands further attention.

HAZING IN MODERN SPORT

Many teams use not only sheer talent, speed, and intelligence to dominate opponents, but also strength, intimidation, and rowdy play to achieve desired victory. This same brutality may also be directed towards co-players in certain instances. Hazing provides an example of how this occurs, creating an environment of intimidation, real or perceived. Current Toronto Maple Leaf President and former all-star goaltender for the Montreal Canadiens, Ken Dryden, has recalled that the pressure of continually waiting to be hazed plagued him for many years after he joined the team in 1971. Despite his tremendous success with the team (six Stanley Cups in a nine-year span), Dryden was haunted "by the ghosts" of the past ready "to get him" (*Fifth estate*, 1996). Mr. Dryden explained, "I was always afraid it was going to happen. I was always sure that when that next year came around and the voices in the dressing room would start to gather and start to say, 'I think we should get ... I think we should get ... that my name would come up ...' If I go through the other side of it, I'm going to feel so humiliated by it that I can't take it. I'm going to go, I'm going to leave. I'll leave hockey" (*Fifth estate*, 1996).

In both Oliver's 1990 book *The making of champions* and Robinson's 1998 book *Crossing the line,* it is clear that hazing occurs in the minor leagues as well. These books document that hazing rituals are a way of life, and sometimes continue even after the dreaded "rookie night" or "hell night." Oliver's book, recounting his experience researching the veteran players of the 1989 WHL Saskatoon Blades, often alludes to hazing practices. As Bryshun mentions in his thesis, although Oliver does not fully detail any hazing ritual except one (Red Rover: a tug-of-war game where the rookie's penises are tied together with a single skate lace), his book suggests that hazing was prevalent during much of the 1989 season (Bryshun, 1997). Oliver further details how veterans always had first-choice seating during bus rides, as well as being served meals first, while the rookies had to carry equipment and were usually debased by small, yet demeaning rituals such as stooping to tie a veteran's shoe when the veteran yelled "shoe check" (Oliver, 1990).

CONCLUSION

Hazing has been a part of academia, religion, and many cultures for generations. Here it has been shown that the early roots of hazing in the educational institution existed for both academic and social reasons. Hazing also has a deeper role in creating power structures wherein those at the top instill a traditional sense of belonging in the weaker members. This tradition may include rough, humiliating, and demeaning treatment. In academia, practices such as these were established to rid a younger student of his "old life" so that he could become part of a group which promised to place him on the path to success—so that he could be welcomed into his new group.

Regardless of the intention of past initiations, athletic hazing practices in current educational settings reveal retrogressive urges and behaviour. In many cases, hazing rituals exploit peer pressure tactics in order to confront, humiliate, and dominate outsiders. If Western hazing traditions were to change, and if they were to cease segregation practices, the new traditions might break down the hierarchical, often patriarchal structure of the group.

By guiding neophytes into a "new life" rather than imposing power structures on them, one could perhaps create groups based on equality and fair play. Yet one thing remains certain: many groups practicing hazing rituals believe they have valid reasons for continuing their traditions. Perhaps they are correct in some instances, perhaps some of these rituals do indeed play a part in the development of young adults in their culture. But while the practice of violent hazing may be somewhat rare, the existence of such violence requires further study and examination. More questions should be asked.

REFERENCES

Bryshun, J. (1997). *Hazing in sport: An exploratory study of veteran/rookie relations.* Unpublished master's thesis, University of Calgary, Calgary, Alberta, Canada.

Donnelly, P. and Young, K. (1988). "The construction and confirmation of identity in sport subcultures," *Sociology of Sport Journal* 5: 223–240.

Dryden, K. (1983). *The game.* Toronto, ON: Macmillan.

Fifth Estate. (1996). *Thin ice.* Canadian Broadcasting Corporation, October 29.

MacIntyre, N. (2001). "Trouble in the hen house," *Argosy* 16: 130.

Maclean's Magazine. (January 30, 1995). "The hell of hazing."

Nuwer, H. (1990). *Broken pledges: The deadly rite of hazing.* Atlanta: Longstreet Press.

Oliver, R. (1990). *The making of champions.* Markham, ON: Penguin.

Robinson, L. (1998). *Crossing the line: Sexual harassment and abuse in Canada's national sport.* Toronto: McClelland and Stewart.

Toohey, D.M. and Swann, C.P. (1985). "A comparative study of North American subcultures," *Comparative Physical Education and Sport* 3: 327–334.

CHAPTER 1

Hazing—A Story

Laura Robinson

Two years after my book *Crossing the line: Violence and sexual assault in Canada's national sport* came out, I was sitting in my favorite café in Canmore, Alberta, before a morning ski. A woman came into the café and recognized me as the author of the book. She complimented me on the book and told me how glad she was that I had written it. I thanked her, chatted for a minute, and then went back to my bagel and newspaper. But I soon felt as if someone were watching me. I looked up. The man at the next table was trying to catch my attention.

"What book did you write?" he asked.

"Oh, a book on hockey," I replied.

"What kind of book on hockey?" he asked back.

I don't usually like to reveal what *Crossing the line* is about because the ensuing conversation normally takes up too much time, and on this particular day I wanted to read the paper and go skiing. "It's about junior hockey," I told him.

"Well, what about it?" came the response.

I could feel the conversation evolving even if I didn't really want it to. "It's about sexual abuse in junior hockey," I said.

"Oh, you mean about that coach in Saskatchewan who sexually abused Sheldon Kennedy."

This is a standard statement I hear when I tell people what the book is about, and I always make sure they understand that only two chapters are about the Graham James case in Swift Current, Saskatchewan. "Actually the Swift Current case is in there, but I was researching for several years before that case hit the news," I said. "Most of my case studies involved alleged gang rape and initiations. I don't believe there are many hockey coaches who are sexual predators like James, but I did find a lot of abuse through team initiations."

"Right, I know what you mean," he said.

"I don't mean just unpleasant things like having your head shaved or being made to do embarrassing things in public," I replied. "I mean really hard-core sado-masochistic torture of boys that is premeditated and ritualistic."

The fellow at the table next to me didn't miss a beat. "I know," he replied, "I was in the American Marines."

And so went yet another typical conversation I have had with countless men since *Crossing the line* came out: men who felt the need to speak to me about their own experiences of sexual abuse, and may never even have called it that until the quite unpleasant can of worms of male-on-male sexual abuse was opened up in Canada in 1990.

A BRIEF HISTORY

This book is about initiation in sport, and this particular chapter will relay some of the stories men told me about initiations once *Crossing the line* was published. I believe that in order to understand where we are now, we must look back on from where we have come. Sexually exploitative initiations are a slice of the big picture and this picture, based on secrecy, homophobia, and intimidation, keeps most athletes who have survived an initiation quiet. The dirty secret is safely hidden. It is because initiations are part of the whole experience of the athlete and part of the canvas on which we paint our own sexualities that I will briefly look at the history of the whole.

Since the women's movement of the 1960s, women have looked critically at notions of sexuality, including the phenomenon of sexual assault, and in so doing have sought to understand, examine, and heal their lives. But in Canada, the sexual abuse of boys was not treated seriously by the media until 1990, when abuse was disclosed at Mount Cashel, the boys' home in Newfoundland run by the Christian Brothers, and subsequently at residential schools by Phil Fontaine, Grand Chief of the Assembly of

Manitoba Chiefs at that time. Men were now speaking the unspeakable: naming the pain and hurt that had so badly interrupted their sexual and human journey.

In the fall of 1996, Sheldon Kennedy became the first high-profile male athlete in Canada to address the issue publicly when he went to the police, who eventually charged his junior hockey coach, Graham James, with 350 counts of sexual abuse. Because Kennedy went public and because he was an NHL player, I believe he readied the sport community for more disclosures about male-on-male sexual abuse.

However, two years before Kennedy came forward, another brave hockey player went to the police in his community. He didn't play in the NHL, but that doesn't mean his contribution to making sport a better place isn't just as important. His name is Scott McLeod, and in 1993 he made the Tilbury Hawks junior C hockey team. What he didn't imagine was that making the team on his skill was not enough. One of the owners of the team had the players over for a party before the season began. At the end of that night, which became a nightmare, Scott walked sixteen kilometers home in the pouring rain. Eventually, he went to the police and 135 sex crime charges were laid against the owners, managers, coaches, trainers, and senior players of the team. They'd put the team through a little initiation—a few games, all in good fun, of course.

The Tilbury Hawk case became a case study in *Crossing the line*. What I found interesting about the reaction to this case was the lack of it. Six rookie players endured a night of sado-masochistic torture, but the *Toronto star* only carried a small item on the sports page when the charges were laid. In Chatham, where the trial was held, it was the court reporter, Bill Currie, who covered the case, not a sportswriter. In fact, in the office of the sports editor were citations and plaques from the local hockey association thanking him for his great support.

Earlier that year, I had met at the Ottawa airport a member of the Airborne Regiment who was just returning from Somalia. Later we would hear about their initiations—inspired by ugly racism, murder, and horrible acts of sexual assault. But when this soldier commenced his description of what his unit liked to do for fun, which included beating one another to a pulp—after all, "someone had to be the cunt," he told me several times, I had not heard of the Tilbury Hawks, nor had the Somalian Airborne scandal occurred yet.

THE JOURNEY CALLED *CROSSING THE LINE*

While researching and writing *Crossing the line*, I thought of this soldier frequently. Over and over again I heard the same theme repeated in hockey, though perhaps not quite so directly. Someone had to be the cunt, the bitch, the girl, the fill-in female whom the real men could penetrate, either literally or symbolically. A rookie player is the best choice, because as Scott McLeod learned, making the team on skill isn't what the Boys' Club is really about. At the end of the initiation, any soft, empathetic, or slightly female side of a male has been cleansed through this theatre of violent masculinity. He emerges as a dutiful killing machine: a man who does what he's told by his superiors and does not question the intent or the ethic. The rookie has entered the world of male violence and aggressive team sport where he is constantly reminded that even the symbolic presence of women is to be denigrated. "You're my bitch for the week," the new player on the team would be told by a senior player when he first joins the team.

Ethnographer Michel Robidoux, in his 2001 book, *Men at play: A working understanding of professional hockey,* notes that if a player does something as simple as bring back a take-out lunch for another player when he goes out to get his own, he is referred to in female terms. "Thanks, bitch," the other player responds when handed lunch. Any act of so-called servitude is seen not only as female, but as female in a derogatory way. Women aren't seen as anything but a negative force in these all-male institutions.

The anecdotes Robidoux reported in his book were similar to what I found during my book tour for *Crossing the line* in 1998, though I was not restricted by the ethical considerations by which academics must abide. If someone started telling me a story, I didn't need to let them know that I was gathering data on the subject matter and that, while their identity would remain anonymous, their story might be chronicled. In many ways, as journalists, if we just listen and let other people fill the empty airspace, we can find out anything we could possibly want to know—and often, things we do not. In addition to the more fluid role journalists are afforded, is the advantage I believe women journalists and researchers have in this area. We do not represent the world that hurt most sexual abuse survivors. We are not representative of maleness, but instead are often seen, if we act with honesty, integrity, and empathy, as coming from the world that the "hurt boy," who is now a man, once knew.

But the presence of women does not guarantee the safety of children. Unfortunately, we have seen evidence of women failing to act with the values for which women are traditionally known. Recently, in Edmonton, Alberta, two hockey coaches were suspended for a year on two separate occasions when they pulled their teams off the ice after they determined that the play was endangering their players. They were exercising "duty of care," an ethical concept that they are legally responsible to exercise as adults in positions of power. The coaches were acting *"in loco parentis"*; in other words, as local parents trying to ensure the well-being of the children for whom they were responsible. The president of the Edmonton Minor Hockey Association, Charlene Davis, toed the party line and declared that coaches couldn't possibly be responsible for the safety of all their athletes. While this parroting of males values is not pervasive amongst women who have achieved positions of power in traditionally male establishments, it is very troubling. The women's liberation movement is not about straight-jacketing ourselves into maleness. Men and women must work together and bring a new set of values that challenge accepted norms.

Fathers of hockey players contacted me after they read *Crossing the line* to let me know about their own battles with hockey associations when they tried to address the legacy of initiations in their son's hockey career, and how frustrated they were with the association's lack of action. Every time a hockey player came forward with a story of abuse, the association couched it as an isolated incident. The perpetrators came from outside of hockey, not from within its charmed circle. The following story, relayed to me by an athlete who played in both the CHL and the NHL, belies this myth.

In 1999, when I spoke at Queen's University in Kingston, a fourth-year physical education student was most interested in meeting with me. He had played in the WHL and went on to a professional career in the NHL, but didn't want to pursue what is seen as a dream life by so many Canadians boys. He pursued sport sociology instead, and had read *Crossing the line*. He shook my hand when I arrived and thanked me for my honesty. "The book would have been worse if I'd written it," he said and proceeded to tell me about the initiations of the Kamloops Blazers, his team in the WHL.

"They made us strip on a road trip in the bus and put us in the sweat-box," he said referring to the tiny bathroom at the back of buses. "One at a time we had to walk down the aisle with our hands behind our heads, stop in front of every player and let them hit our genitals with whatever object they felt like using. I was a pretty quiet guy, not in your face, so I didn't get it bad, but there was one guy who was a real loudmouth. They could use anything—coat hangers, cassette cases. They made him bleed. We had to go all the way to the front of the bus. That's where the coach was, and he was laughing. Now he coaches in the NHL."

This player lived at home and believed his parents would have supported him if he'd spoken out. They weren't typical hockey parents, pushing their son in order to bask in his glory. But to that day he hadn't told them. There is such a taboo about "going against the team" that even a player with supportive parents, who is not wedded to the hockey dream himself, didn't tell. Eventually, though, he did write his fourth-year major paper on initiations in hockey.

There may be great pressure to keep the secret, but as we allow for honesty and create a supportive climate, there is often a more overwhelming need to disclose. In the fall of 1998 I was on the evening FAN radio talk show discussing *Crossing the line*. A caller phoned in with a dilemma that was causing him great pain. His cousin's son had made a junior hockey team, he said, but he didn't know how to tell him what was in store for him.

"What do you mean, what is in store for him?" the host asked.

"I played junior hockey. I mean the initiations," he said. "They told me we were having a team party and to be at this guy's address at a certain time. I showed up and right from the front door they dragged me and pushed me downstairs. They told me to take all my clothes off and if I didn't, they'd do stuff to me that was even worse than if I cooperated. I did what they wanted and it was really horrible. I don't know how to tell my cousin's son about it."

The caller was very emotional, and I asked him if he had told anyone about what had happened to him. "No," he said, "not even my dad, but I am now because I know he's listening."

The evening turned out to be emotional for everyone. Another father, one whose son's story was chronicled in *Crossing the line*, called in to give support. It soon became clear to me that, just like women, men all over the world were walking wounded. But unlike women, who have spent the last four decades talking about their wounds and creating spaces in which they can heal and move on, men, until very recently, have stoically suffered in silence. As I mentioned above, it is the secrecy created by the pseudo-religious mystique of the locker room, homophobia, and intimidation that has kept men in sport silent for so long.

Intimidation, both on and off the ice, plays a crucial role in keeping players quiet about initiations and other forms of abuse. In his 1998 book, *Real boys: Rescuing our sons from the myths of boyhood*, American clinical psychologist William Pollack argues that boys are raised to understand intimidation as a way of helping them become real men. He gives an example of how boys learn at such a young age to submit to intimidation, and consequently receive positive feedback for their submissiveness:

Doug's five-year-old Tommy was skating at his daughter's mainly female skating class. He was unsteady on his feet, and his knee started to bleed after his fourth tumble. Pollack observes that Tommy "sought his father's solace, near the visitor's gallery. 'No more today, Dad,' Tommy pleaded, 'My knee really hurts!'

'Nah … that doesn't hurt too much,' his dad replied. 'C'mon, keep going. You're not going to let a bunch of girls beat you out of the competition are you?'"

Later on, Tommy gets inadvertently smashed between two teenage girls, but still his father insists he continue. A year passes. When Pollack sees Tommy again, he is playing hockey: "As Tommy maneuvered the puck toward the opposing team's goal, three much larger boys rammed into him from all angles. When Tommy began to lose his balance, one of the boys helped him finish the fall, shoving little Tommy onto the ice."

Tommy has learned by now how to submit to pain and to the performance expected by his father. Pollack writes, "His skating now significantly improved, Tommy raced after the opponents with abandon. As he approached the kid who had pushed him, Tommy skated even faster. When their two bodies collided almost head-on, his opponent went flying against the side board with a forceful bang.

"Thatta boy!" yelled Tommy's father, and gave him a two-fist salute (Pollack, 1998: 286–88).

Unfortunately, this is a familiar story, played out on every rink in every community across North America. Boys, desperate for the approval of their fathers and later, father figures such as coaches and team managers, submit to intimidation that runs from subtle to violent. Subtle intimidation occurs when someone taunts boys, to get them to do something about which they may be hesitant. In sport the taunts are most often the kind Tommy's father used. They compare boys and men to girls, women, and "fags," and ask the boy if perhaps he has switched into a different category of sexuality, simply because of his hesitation. Because sport, particularly aggressive male team sport, is so misogynistic and homophobic, the boy risks being seen as "not a man" if he doesn't do what is requested of him.

This breaking down of the autonomy of self takes place over years, and is combined with much worse intimidation. One junior team on which I reported told their rookie players if they didn't submit to the initiation, part of which involved skating with marshmallows in their rectums and after practice shitting them out and eating them, they would have much worse done to them during the season. Again, the autonomous institution of the team and management of the team virtually assured compliance. Even the team doctor—someone the boys should be able to go to in confidence about the behaviour of teammates—was also a major owner of the team, which is a clear conflict of interest. A doctor's responsibility is to ensure the good health of people at all times, at all costs. An owner of a hockey team's responsibility is to put a product out there that doesn't just win on the ice, but wins with the public too. He has a vested interest in keeping dirty secrets hidden.

As players come of age in junior hockey, their own fathers are replaced by other important father figures, such as coaches, owners, general managers, and those high up in hockey administration. In the case of the Guelph Storm, another team I investigated for *Crossing the line,* the principal of the school most of the players attended was also the president of the hockey club.

When a girl went to the police about a gang rape she alleged the team committed against her, she also felt the need to switch schools. In her eyes, she could not trust the educational institution she attended when the administration had such a strong affiliation with the hockey club. Whether it was a player who wanted to report an initiation to a coach, or a girl who wanted to continue her education in an unbiased environment, this hierarchy of men, who have powerful and insidious ways of affecting a young person's future, act as the gate-keepers in this intimidation game. An athlete could not comfortably speak out against the traditions of initiation any more than a girl could about rape by one of their boys. What is important to realize is that it is the perception of the young person that counts in these cases. Both men, the principal and the coach in this instance, can act in a professional manner and not exploit their positions; however, if a young person feels vulnerable and unable to disclose information, then harm has been done. It is for this reason that there are conflict-of-interest rules. If team doctors do not become owners of teams, and school principals do not become team presidents, young people, both on the team and those who come in contact with the team, may more readily disclose distressful information involving the team.

The intimidation used by the players on the ice is much more straightforward and easier to understand: do as I say or pay the consequences for the rest of the season. While the ice can be used as a stage for public intimidation, initiations are within the team, and in public, the team must appear to be a cohesive unit. Intimidation must remain in the locker room, and in what sport sociologist Dr. Steven Ortiz of Oregon State calls "the mobile total institution" as the team moves from arena to arena. The town may change, but the locker room remains the same. Breaking secrecy codes is tantamount to treason, and with only one exit that is easily blocked, the locker room provides the perfect setting for coercion and intimidation.

Ortiz also argues that the locker-room code is so mobile that other sites can be substituted for the locker room, as long as members of the team are present. This is why so many of the alleged gang rapes and initiations in *Crossing the line* happened in basements, and why garages and buses could also be utilized for initiations. All three locations can easily trap an unsuspecting player or fan, who can exercise little recourse through their physical environment.

The other phenomenon people brought to my attention was the commonplaceness of the rape and gang rape of girls and young women by junior hockey players. The very first story that tweaked my interest in sexual abuse in junior hockey had been an alleged gang rape case in Swift Current, Saskatchewan, in 1989. Once I had investigated it, I had to find out if Swift Current was a particularly sick place or if there was a rape culture in junior hockey. After finishing the research for *Crossing the line*, I realized that junior hockey has a rape culture, and that Swift Current was a troubled community. After listening to the stories of both rape and initiations in hockey, I now believe the two are inextricably tangled up together in a dangerous and symbiotic relationship. I will address this relationship later on in this chapter, but for now I would like to give an example of the blasé attitude people steeped in junior hockey culture have towards both.

One male journalist, disgusted with a reprehensible sexual act that he witnessed, failed to intervene in defense of the girl who was victimized by the actions. Nor did he tell the players that the way they were treating her was reprehensible. There was an acceptance of such behaviour and an expectation that it exists as part of the male sport culture. Similarly, there was a belief in the inevitability of perverse acts in initiations.

I remember driving to a northern community with another ski instructor, a young man who was barely twenty. He told me about his involvement in sport, and that he had dropped out of midget rec hockey and was lucky he had found skiing. Why did you drop out of hockey? I asked.

"I don't know," he said, "they just weren't very nice."

"What wasn't nice?"

"I didn't like what they made me do."

"What did they make you do?"

"Oh nothing really, but I had to take my clothes off at a party and they shaved me. You know, they shaved my genitals. I just didn't feel like sticking around any more."

"That sounds pretty bad."

"I didn't care. I just didn't feel like playing."

I waited for a while and he didn't offer anything more.

"That was a sexual assault that occurred," I said.

"No, it wasn't," he replied. "It was at a party."

"On the way to the party did you say to yourself, 'gee I hope someone makes me get undressed and then shaves my genitals?'"

"No, I thought it was sick," he said. "I never thought about it again until now. Ya, I couldn't believe they wanted to do it, but we were drinking, so I went along, but I didn't want to play after that."

And so my conversations with boys and young men went, and continued. The more I heard stories like these, the more five areas of research became apparent. First of all, there is a secret, sad, and very disturbing culture in hockey, and probably in other sports as well, that is much larger than I had imagined while researching and writing *Crossing the line*. Secondly, the correlation between gang rapes and initiations needs much more investigation. Thirdly, in this line, we must also investigate the relationship between male privilege in sport and the rape of girls and women by male sport teams. What relationship is there between keeping hockey predominantly male (by allocating ice-time, coaching staff, programs, arena budgets, and media attention mainly to them), and those privileged players' practice of initiation rituals and gang rapes? Fourthly, there are millions of men who have survived sports teams, the military, private boy's schools, gangs, and religious institutions all over the world who have terrible memories of initiations and rapes in which they were either the perpetrator, the victim, or both, and virtually none had any professional counseling. Finally, despite the terrible nature of these actions, for the most part, the men and boys who reported them to me did so with complete nonchalance. I believe such acts are seen as acceptable behaviour in the never-ending quest to prove masculinity in the twisted subcultures of hockey and other hypermasculine institutions. What happens to the psyche, particularly the sexual psyche, of massive numbers of boys and men who normalize sexually degrading, violent, humiliating actions?

I'd like to go through these areas one by one to better explain why I believe much more research is necessary. Outsiders to junior hockey are often shocked by the behaviour of players and coaches. There is a very different ethos on the bus, in the locker room, and at parties than there is at official team and league functions where the players act in extraordinarily polite ways, knowing the team's PR man is watching. Let me say as well that not all players have this inside/outside behaviour. There are many who are fine boys and young men until their loyalty to the team is tested. One must not forget, for instance, that of the 26 players on the Swift Current Broncos in 1994 who knew that coach Graham James was assaulting at least one of their teammates, only two stood up and would not play for James. Darren McLean and Kevin Powell categorically refused to play if James was the coach, while every single other player agreed to play, despite knowledge of his criminal behaviour. I also recall the case study I did in *Crossing the line* on the Tilbury Hawks Junior C team. Six rookie players were initiated at a team owner's house. The initiation included several sado-masochistic games the boys were to play with each other while the owners, coaches, trainers, manager, and senior players sat in a semi-circle and watched them. The rookie players, all of whom were underage, were made to drink copious amounts of alcohol as well.

After one of the rookie players, Scott McLeod, went to the police about the initiations, 135 sex crime charges were laid. But of the six players only McLeod and one other player would cooperate with police. The other four were described by Crown Attorney Paul Bailey as hostile witnesses, who said that they willingly allowed grown men to sit nude on their faces and were happy to drink beer that had had penises dipped in it. This assault was also premeditated. The garage into which the boys were brought was set up with a semi-circle of chairs and the equipment needed for the "games" they were going to play. At one point as Bailey prepared for the case, a senior lawyer from the region called him and asked him what the big deal was. It was only a hockey initiation, he said, not a criminal act.

Even the best-laid physical plans, such as those of the Tilbury Hawks, won't have any long-term success if there isn't an emotional threat. The fear of homosexuality permeates male team sports even more than other aspects of our culture. In his book, *Don't tell: The sexual abuse of young boys*, counselor Michel Forais argues that boys learn there is only one kind of man, and unless they take the correct path to that manhood, they will never be men. A man, says Forais, is in charge; therefore, when a boy finds himself being abused, he is obviously not masculine material. He is still just a child because it is he who plays the submissive role. This is the first way in which he feels shame. But, if he is not a man, then who is he? The only people who are penetrated (I use this word literally and symbolically) by men are women and gays. The other edge of the homophobia sword is misogyny, which is particularly vicious in male team sport where "being a girl" is greatly feared.

Misogynistic logic is used in military initiations, as soldiers not only physically penetrate new recruits in some instances, but like junior hockey players, refer to rookies as girls who "need to have their curls cut off" and "have had abortions." (Robinson, 1998: 93). Most recently, the Canadian Forces Base in Winnipeg was investigated after soldiers who were suffering from Post Traumatic Stress Syndrome from duty in the Middle East, Afghanistan, or Kosovo tried to get help on the base. In the annual parade the base hosts, these men were depicted as women/transsexuals who were imprisoned in a pink cage on a float that had the initials CT on it. Going to the other side of the base to see a counselor was known as getting on the CT or Crazy Train. These symbols were further entrenched in miso-gynistic symbolism by the other meaning of CT, which is Cock Tease. Any admission of "weakness," or evidence that a soldier's life is anything but exemplary, is retaliated against in the private/public environment of the base. Pain is not acknowledged and those who mention it are ostracized and feminized in sport and the military.

This fear silences almost all victims in initiations and other forms of sexual abuse. The paradox of homophobia in male sport, particularly male team sport, is that it is manifested in a highly homoerotic culture. This is a culture that worships the young, male body for its physical prowess. As I mentioned above, men buy, sell, and trade boys and young men in junior hockey for these qualities. Many would argue that the only difference between junior hockey and the boy stroll of any city is that in hockey, a vicarious sexuality is being sold, while on the stroll, it's quite clear—boys are being sold to men for physical sex.

While covering the preliminary hearing that investigated the initiation rituals of the Tilbury Hawks, I observed the owners, managers, trainers, and coaches of the team during Scott McLeod's testimony in the Chatham, Ontario courtroom. Before the hearing began, each man walked into the room with his wife walking dutifully behind him. Given that these were male-on-male sexual abuse charges, it was important, even before the first oath was taken, that the men establish traditional heterosexuality. A woman needed to be present, but she also had to play a subservient role. She could not be acting as a lawyer for the defendants, or be a fellow hockey coach. The women who belong to these men can only be wives, and wives who are willing to walk and sit behind their men.

While Scott gave his testimony, I watched the hockey men. They started to inch up in their seats, and before long, as Scott gave details about how one of them put on surgical gloves to insert marshmallows in the boys' rectums, their faces broke into grins, and they sat on the edge of their seats. It appeared that they were very excited over Scott's descriptions.

When we find an ethos that represses sexuality and sees sexuality— particularly female sexuality (as mentioned above, the rookies are the designated females for the night) as dirty—we find deeply entrenched and highly secretive sexual abuse. When men have inordinate amounts of power in cultures that define masculinity in terms of power, intimidation, and traditional heterosexuality, we find multi-layered webs of denial and cover-ups. We set up a perfect example of how a rape culture flourishes.

I believe there is a relationship between the alleged initiations I researched and the alleged gang rapes I also investigated in junior hockey. All the aspects of a culture that allow initiations to flourish, many of which are manifested through rape, allow gang rape to occur. In November 2002, I delivered a paper on my research in junior hockey to the *Play the game* conference in Copenhagen, Denmark. The conference was for media professionals in a globalized sport world, and the theme was, "Who has the power?" I spoke about the difficulties involved not only in writing about such deep pain in young people, but also in coming up against the power machine in Canada that protects, at all costs, the public image of hockey. Afterwards, men from African countries and from the former Yugoslavia spoke with me. During war, they had seen gang rapes because soldiers considered women's bodies as part of the property they seized. But they hadn't spoken about it, they said, until I talked about Canadian hockey.

What happens when the initiation rituals or the locker-room practices are examined with women's eyes? We question everything that has normally been taken for granted. This is not because, as I mentioned earlier, we are superior moral beings compared to men, but because the culture of women is profoundly different than that of men.

I have been an athlete since 1972 in sports that have traditionally been seen as male. Bicycle racing has long and chauvinistic roots in Europe, as does rowing, which has even longer, and far more elitist roots. Cycling did not become an event for women at the Olympics until 1984, while women's rowing first appeared in 1976. The Argonaut Rowing Club in Toronto did not open its doors to women until 1981, and women's cycling is still very much a poor cousin to men's cycling in elite racing. My winter sport of Nordic skiing was probably the only sport of the three in which I competed that had any historical models of egalitarianism. Still, for all the macho culture to which women athletes in these sports were exposed, we did not adopt the male cultural values associated with the locker room. Never have I been in a women's locker room, either as an athlete or journalist, and witnessed anything close to the typical posturing and promenading that is exhibited in men's locker rooms inhabited by competitive team sport athletes.

As a sports journalist, I am frequently amazed at what my male colleagues do not see. While I have always felt at home covering Nordic skiing or any sport at the Summer Olympics, when I enter the hockey arena, I feel like an outsider. As I walk down the Hall of Fame—the foyer and hallway of virtually every Canadian hockey arena—I see trophies, plaques, banners, and photos that commemorate the history of the white males who play this sport. This is a rather exclusive depiction of history, considering they make up a minority of the population. There are so few hours of ice-time given to women's and girls' teams that I have only once walked into an arena and unexpectedly seen females on the ice. It is an atmosphere that does not reflect women or women's values.

In 1993, when I covered the Memorial Cup in Sault Saint Marie because the Sault Greyhound's star player was up on a sexual assault charge, I watched, not the players, but the girls and young women in the stands and hallways after the home team won the championship. While my male colleagues interviewed the winning young men, I saw the angry sizing-up that was going on between the girls in the hallways. On the one hand were the players' hometown girlfriends who stood in the corridors that led to the locker rooms. On the other were the girls in the stands who did not have this coveted status. Girlfriends, who had traveled from the players' hometowns to the Sault, and local girls, who hoped for girlfriend status, knew they were in competition for the attention of these star athletes. They shot nasty bolts at one another because all wondered the same thing: would the star player take his hometown girlfriend to the celebrations, or arrange to meet secretly later with the girl he'd been having sex with while playing for the Greyhounds? Or would he choose a new girl altogether if she was lucky enough to catch his eye on this very important night? Like their boyfriends on the team who need to catch the eye of the NHL scout watching their game and to play aggressively enough to win his attention, so these girls must learn how to catch the eye of the hockey player. Because of the gendered nature of relationships in the arena, boys don't gain points unless they are aggressive on ice, while girls must stay off the ice to gain points and transform themselves into whatever it is they believe male hockey players want. These games of sexuality, whether they are about proving masculinity through aggression on ice, in the locker room afterwards, or about proving femininity by waiting patiently until men are finished performing, are the most fundamental story of Canadian hockey. For whatever reason, male journalists either do not see these sexual games, or these games are so deeply entrenched in the gendered nature of sport themselves that journalists can't step back to critically examine what is before them, as journalists are supposed to do.

What does this lack of vision have to do with initiations in hockey? First of all, as stated earlier, just as women are not genetically predisposed to having higher morals than males, not all men wear blinders. It is important to note that male journalists outside of the sporting arena have written insightful critiques of the hockey culture. During the Tilbury Hawks case, Bill Currie of the *Chatham daily news* wrote extensively and intelligently about what the story was really about. Meanwhile, the sports section of the newspaper barely acknowledged the scandal, though the editor at the time proudly displayed, in his office, the plaque the local hockey association had given him for his great support. He also argued once that marshmallows were not fully inserted into the boys' rectums, but rather, "just between the cheeks."

In the January 1998 edition of *Harper's magazine,* Canadian writer Guy Lawson wrote of the Flin Flon Bombers, a provincial level junior hockey team. In "Hockey Nights: The tough skate through junior-league life," Lawson looks at the rough and difficult life of a northern town, and the equally rough hockey played in that town. Unlike most Canadian sports writers, he generally stays away from romanticizing the game and players, and writes about one player who must testify soon against two friends in Regina who are up on sexual assault and murder charges. A letter to the editor from a resident of Flin Flon gives a good example of what Canadians normally expect from media coverage of hockey:

> Guy Lawson's article about hockey in Flin Flon had nothing to do with hockey and our tremendous love and appreciation for the sport. His portrayal made our town look horrible. Where does Lawson get off talking about LSD, prostitution, and other things that have nothing to do with hockey? Flin Flon is very famous for hockey, yet there is very little about it in the article. I suspect that Lawson is not even a hockey fan.
> —Georgina Switzer, Flin Flon, Manitoba

While Lawson ruffled feathers in Flin Flon, another letter from a former junior player in April 1998 gives us an idea of what Lawson may have missed. I will let the former junior player end this chapter in his own words:

> Like Lawson, I played hockey (in British Columbia) before I gave up on the narrow road to the Canadian male mecca, a professional career in hockey. What's noticeably absent from Lawson's account, however, is any mention of the secret sadistic rituals of rookie initiation. Perhaps Lawson didn't stick around in Flin Flon long enough to witness it, or maybe it is less prevalent nowadays, but I am inclined to think that he simply didn't get the whole story.

When I was playing in the early 1980s, the brutality perpetrated in one's own dressing room rivaled what Lawson describes on the ice. For example, after a practice it was not unusual to find a rookie player suddenly and violently subdued, stripped naked, and taped to a crucifix made of hockey sticks. He might then have his eyebrows, head, chest, legs, armpits, and pubic hair shaved so indelicately that it left him bleeding. Players in this prone position were spit and pissed on, spray-painted, and threatened with shit. Heet, an ointment for aching muscles, was ludicrously applied to their testicles, which after being shaved is nothing short of torture.

On one occasion, I saw a smoking cigar pushed into the rectum of a player (probings with the butt end of a stick were not unusual); and on another, a hot-water enema was crudely administered using a water bottle. The player, who fought this invasion valiantly, was badly scalded but at least his bowels were spared.

Finally, there was the "cracker race." Run like a conventional relay race, the naked rookies were organized into teams and an obstacle course established. The baton in this instance, however, was a Ritz cracker that was inserted in the cleft of one player's sweaty ass and handed off, after running the course, by removing it with one's lips and inserting it into one's own sweaty ass. Breaking or dropping the cracker during the race resulted in the horror of having to eat it and start over. Losing the race meant eating the other team's cracker.

My guess is that Lawson experienced some form of this abuse when he played, and that it went on in Flin Flon as well. If not, then bleak as Canadian junior hockey seems, it reflects an improvement over what it was a few years ago.

—Robert Giannetto, New York City

REFERENCES

Forais, M. (2002). *Don't tell: The sexual abuse of young boys.* Montreal: McGill-Queen's University Press.

Lawson, G. (January 1998). "Letters to the Editor," *Harper's magazine* 296(155).

Pollack, W. (1998). *Rescuing our sons from the myths of boyhood.* New York: Random House.

Robidoux, M. (2001). *Men at play: A working understanding of professional hockey.* Montreal: McGill-Queen's University Press.

Robinson, L. (1998). *Crossing the line: Violence and sexual assault in Canada's national sport.* Toronto: McClelland and Stewart.

CHAPTER 2

Hazing—What the Law Says

R. Brian Crow and Dennis R. Phillips

The purpose of this chapter is to address the legal implications of hazing in athletics, U.S. statutory laws, successful and unsuccessful prosecution and defenses for hazing, and outline specific anti-hazing policies in force in some sport settings. Secondarily, the authors will examine the prevalence of hazing in sport while highlighting specific recent media coverage.

SCOPE OF HAZING IN ATHLETICS

The prevalence of hazing in athletics is difficult to accurately document for several reasons. Foremost among them is the reticence of both victims and perpetrators of hazing to acknowledge their participation and role in the activity. Another factor leading to the possible under-representation of athletic hazing incidents is that student-athletes, coaches, and administrators seem to not fully comprehend the broad definition of hazing and its consequences (Hoover, 1999).

Hazing has become an almost routine occurrence on college and university campuses. It is most frequently associated with fraternal organizations as a ritual part of the membership process. However, in recent years, the media has covered widespread hazing incidents involving athletic teams at both the high school and college levels. The amount of hazing in recreation and sport is unknown, however, due to the probable large number of unreported cases. Regardless of the total number of incidents, the amount reported has grown dramatically during the past twenty years. The seriousness of the physical and emotional harm has led law officials to prosecute involved student-athletes, and to hold accountable school administrators and coaches for the safety of those entrusted to them in school activities. Prosecution is most often based on state anti-hazing statutes that vary greatly in definition, degree, and scope of penalty. Statutes differ from state to state in their definition of what constitutes hazing actions. They frequently differ in classification of crime and in the degree of severity associated with the criminal action. They also carry a diverse course of punitive and management action for the perpetrators, and compensation and recourse for the victims. Athletic hazing can involve benign initiation-rite activities which have rookie members perform mundane chores such as cleaning locker rooms, carrying equipment bags, collecting food trays following team meals, and singing team "fight" songs. Hazing can also involve such dangerous and illegal activities as binge drinking, sexual harassment and abuse, kidnapping, and infliction of pain and torture.

MEDIA COVERAGE

Hazing in sport has received widespread media attention since the late 1990s. Although evidence shows that athletic hazing has been practiced for decades (www.hazing.hanknuwer.com), only recently has mainstream U.S. media begun publicizing many of the incidents. For example, in 2002, Home Box Office's *Real sports with Bryant Gumbel* presented a story about athletic hazing that received national acclaim (HBO, July 23, 2002). ESPN, in 2000, developed a five-part series (April 10–14) for its highly acclaimed news series *Outside the lines,* examining initiation activities in sport and offering suggestions for when these activities get out of control and become hazing (www.espn.go.com/otl/hazing/monday.html). In addition, Cable News Network (CNN) and the American Broadcasting Company (ABC) have both aired stories about the atrocities of hazing in athletics.

The academic literature has been relatively silent regarding hazing in sport, with the recent exception of two law review articles (Rosner and Crow, 2002; Crow and Rosner, 2002) and work in Canada by Findlay (1998). Hank Nuwer, an anti-hazing advocate and author of several books on hazing, has devoted a portion of the revenue from some of his work to stopping hazing in athletics. Nuwer has also developed a website (www.stophazing.org) dedicated to the dissemination of information about the consequences of hazing in a variety of settings (academic, military, fraternity and sorority, and athletic).

U.S. HAZING LAWS

Most hazing incidents in the United States involve civil rather than criminal charges. Victims often sue the perpetrators, the school district, and its employees under various state and federal statutes (Rosner and Crow, 2002).

State Statutes

Prosecutors face many difficulties in charging those accused of illegal hazing. One is the definition of the activity. An overly broad definition may encompass relatively harmless activities that might not warrant the necessary time and expense to prosecute. A too narrow definition might "handcuff" prosecutors in their pursuit of justice. Some definitions only apply to institutions of higher education and exclude secondary schools, while others exclude athletic teams. Still others allow only for hazing during pre-initiation or actual initiation activities, and do not cover post-initiation events. These concerns are also addressed later in the discussion about anti-hazing policy development. Some state law definitions consider the amount of physical injury to be a determinant of actual hazing (Crouch, 1995).

There are a variety of activities specifically listed in the state statutes that point to the difficulty in writing a comprehensive law that effectively deals with the entire problem. Texas statutes on hazing are the most complete, detailed, and lengthy, with separate divisions for personal and organizational hazing and definition of pledging. The New York statute is the shortest, with the description but two sentences in length. Reviewing each statute also points out the lack of uniformity in the wording of various state laws. For example, the Arkansas statute lists such actions as threatening, disgrace, striking, beating, bruising, maiming, and causing feelings of guilt. California law includes personal degradation and physical or mental harm. Connecticut and Idaho provisions include nudity, obscene or indecent exposure involved in hazing activities. Delaware lists destruction of private or public property, whipping, branding, and forced calisthenics. Utah law addresses such prohibited student conduct as profanity, substance abuse, assault, cruelty to animals, and electrical shock. North Carolina anti-hazing activities include scolding, frightening, and abusive tricks. Some states, such as Idaho, include forced transportation and abandonment in its list of illegal activities. Colorado and several other states add forced consumption of food, beverage, medication, and controlled substances, as well as sleep, food or fluid deprivation.

Consent is an issue in many states as a determinant of whether hazing has indeed taken place. In some states, a victim's consent or voluntary participation can be used as a defense. However, in over twenty-five states, the laws are specifically written so that the victim's implied or expressed consent to be involved in initiation activities may not be used as a defense by the accused (Rosner and Crow, 2002). Legislators apparently believe that victims are often unaware of the activities in which they will be forced to engage, and/or often succumb to intense peer pressure. For a complete discussion of state hazing statutes, see www.stophazing.org/laws.

Penalties and Punishment

The majority of states classify illegal hazing as a "Misdemeanor" of various degree listed as either "A", "B", "C", or "1st", "2nd", or "3rd". The difference is usually predicated upon such factors as the amount of physical harm, whether a vehicle was involved, whether animals were used and abused, and/or whether the activity was reported by supervisory personnel or not. Activities that fall under the more serious levels of misdemeanor illegality ("A", or "1st" degree) are, in turn, raised to the level of felony classification if the situation involved more serious injuries, death, or use of a dangerous weapon. Penalties become more severe as the level of misdemeanor or felony increase.

Anti-hazing laws provide for a wide range of punishments. The penalties vary as widely from state to state as do the definition and list of activities that constitute illegal hazing. The lack of uniformity in statutory provisions among various states is reflected in monetary fines ranging from $0 to $10,000. Delaware and Florida, for example, have no defined limits for fines. Jail sentencing guidelines also vary widely from ten days up to a year.

Louisiana has the lightest fine guidelines of $10 to $100 and ten to thirty days of incarceration; however, if the incident occurs in a university setting, the perpetrator faces expulsion for at least one school term. Nebraska allows for the stiffest fines of up to $10,000 for a Class II Misdemeanor. Vermont law has a tort limit of $5,000 for civil cases. The most common punishment, however, is a $1,000 fine, three to twelve months of incarceration, or both (Crow, 2001).

Management Provisions and Discipline

Anti-hazing laws also contain management standards that provide penalties for organizations that support hazing, fail to educate about or develop policies against hazing, or are negligent in the supervision of activities involving those they are legally bound to protect and oversee. Alabama and Washington laws provide for scholarship, awards, and entitlement and grant funding to be forfeited if activities are allowed to exist. Arizona, Delaware, Kentucky, Missouri, Minnesota, Tennessee, and other states require universities and school districts to develop written guidelines and policies for defining, identifying, reporting, and punishing hazing. The discipline usually involves suspension, expulsion, withholding of diplomas, and reporting any criminal incidents to local law enforcement authorities. Arizona and Texas laws specify that teachers and staff will be subject to discipline for condoning or failing to report incidents of hazing.

Federal Laws Used to Prosecute Hazing

Federal Constitutional Law precepts are occasionally used in the prosecution of hazing incidents. Deprivation of individual rights is an argument used against school districts to obtain monetary or injunctive relief under 42 section of the United States Code (42 U.S.C. 1983 N55). A student's right to bodily integrity is a constitutionally protected right guaranteed in the Fourth and Fourteenth Amendments, and victims of athletic hazing may argue that they have been deprived of those rights, must be shown that schools have acted intentionally indifferent concerning known or foreseen instances of hazing.

Title IX of the Education Amendments Act of 1972 prohibits discrimination in education programs and activities receiving federal funding.

Victims of alleged sexual abuse have used this federal act in hazing cases during initiation rites. The focus of the argument is on sexual harassment in the realm of what the Supreme Court has defined as "hostile environment." When a hazing act denies an individual the opportunity for participation, it may be viewed as discriminatory. Furthermore, if the school is aware, or should be aware, of such discriminatory or harassing practices towards those who are under their legal disciplinary control, then they may be held responsible in court. Usually a single incident is not sufficient to prove sexual harassment in cases of hazing; however, the continued existence of hazing may give grounds for such an argument by the plaintiffs.

Civil Prosecution

State claims against school authorities or school districts usually include such doctrines as *"in loco parentis"* (in place of the parents), which establishes the school's responsibility for maintaining the degree of welfare and safety normally afforded by a parent. By not protecting students in activities usually considered school-sponsored or -controlled, such as athletic teams, then a school may be held liable for acts of negligent supervision. The school also has a responsibility to maintain order and prevent physical attacks by other students. In order for school personnel to be held liable for hazing incidents, however, it usually must be proven that the hazing incident was foreseeable. Prior knowledge and foreseeability are often difficult to prove, however, and several states have included a mandatory written policy by educational entities in their hazing laws that may indicate that schools are aware of the problem and have addressed the issue with an preemptive strategy, and that therefore such incidents have been foreseeable.

Legal Defense Methods

There are usually three legal doctrines that defense attorneys utilize as arguments for their clients in hazing incidents at educational institutions: Assumption of Risk, Comparative Negligence, and Immunity. Assumption of Risk is an age-old view that all participants assume a certain level of risk involved in physical activities. However, the Assumption of Risk doctrine usually applies only to those risks inherent in the game or within the normal process and rules of the activity. Certainly the risks of physical injury in hazing initiation rites or traditions cannot be considered an inherent part of any organized athletic endeavor, even if the knowledge or threat of such activities exists.

The courts often view Comparative Negligence standards, the second defense principle, as mutual negligence by the plaintiffs and the defendants. The degree to which each is negligent is often a determining factor in the amount of monetary remedy in settling the case. However, the victim can only be viewed as negligent if they are seen as a voluntary and willing participant who expressed or implied consent in being hazed. A majority of states have rejected the consent argument in the written provisions of their anti-hazing legislation.

The third defense principle utilized frequently in hazing cases is the doctrine of Immunity. School personnel often argue that they should be immune from individual acts due to protection of state laws governing state employees. However, the pendulum of court decisions in recent years has swung more to individual accountability in cases involving personal injury due to negligence in schools. Teachers and coaches can no longer hide under the umbrella of immunity protection for their lack of supervision, foreseeability, investigation, or reporting of athletic incidents of hazing.

CANADIAN LAW

Unlike law in the United States, Canadian law does not address the issue of hazing within legislation. An individual who felt victimized by incidents arising from a hazing event, and sought to prosecute those involved, would do so within the laws that apply to non-hazing violations. For example, an individual would prosecute based upon assault and battery or harassment. Another legal approach that could be applied in many cases of hazing would incorporate laws associated with underage alcohol use. Charges could be laid against those who provide alcohol to teammates who have not yet reached legal age for alcohol consumption.

A third, which has significance for the sport organization, is negligence, based upon the assumption that individuals will behave in a way that protects others from an unreasonable risk of harm. Negligence occurs when a duty of care is owed, the standard of care associated with this duty is breached, injury (harm) occurs, and the breach in the standard of care has contributed to the harm incurred. Most would agree that a sport organization has a duty of care for the athletes within its program. Recently, the standard of care includes policy on hazing and its implementation.

In a 1997 case, *MacMillan Bloedel Limited* v. *IWA-Canada, Local 363*, the issue of harassment as a form of initiation was challenged. A female employee of MacMillan Bloedel Limited filed two grievances of sexual harassment with the IWA union following repeated harassment by male co-workers. The complainant alleged that the male employees urinated near her, used vulgar language, exposed themselves to her in the form of mooning, and displayed graffiti about the complainant and her sexuality. The respondents had indicated that their behaviour was part of the initiation of the complainant, serving as a way to have her fit in with the veteran employees. The behaviour continued even after the complainant reported the behaviours to the foreman. The response from the employer resulted in the termination of the respondents. The case went before the courts when the union argued that the terminations were excessive punishments. The outcome of legal action was the termination of one employee and reinstatement of the others with suspensions for the actions recorded in their employment files.

This case has implications for sport organizations. The behaviours exhibited in this case of initiation are typical of those used in sport hazing. The difference is that hazing in sport is more typically a same-sex inter-action, especially in team sports where the extremes of hazing rituals are frequently reported. Second, hazing can be considered harassment, which is a form of discrimination according to the law. In this particular case, the harassment is further identified as sexual harassment. Typically, many of the behaviours in sport hazing have sexual overtones that may fall within this category. And third, the employer (sport organization) was forced to deal with a serious conflict when it might have been resolved with earlier intervention through policy and education.

In the case of a hazing incident that resulted in harm to an athlete, a sport organization may be named for breach of duty, vicarious liability, or contributory negligence. In turn, they might seek defense based upon no breach in duty, or voluntary assumption of risk/consent. As noted within the American legislation, consent can be used as a defense in some juris-dictions only. With the Canadian approach, consent does not provide a defense for the commission of an illegal act. Individuals who provide alcohol to those who have not yet reached the legal age for its consumption cannot defend their actions based upon the consent of a minor. Other issues that might render consent illegitimate in cases of sport hazing would be coercion, group consent, and consent to the unknown. Although not yet tested in a court of law, consent would be unlikely to serve a respondent well as a defense in a case involving hazing. Individuals cannot provide consent for others to contravene the law.

A case in point, although again not sport related, occurred in 1999. Hazing rituals for new employees at a Canadian Tire store were common. In this particular case, a teenager was accidentally set on fire by fellow employees. The lawsuit alleges that "there was a hazing ritual or prank engaged in by employees and managerial and supervisory staff at the Canadian Tire Store whereby gas-line anti-freeze or other liquid substances would be poured onto another employee in order to surprise, frighten and cause discomfort." When the complainant was subjected to this behaviour, a lighter sparked, and, fuelled by the liquids, set his pants on fire. The lawsuit claims negligence and breaches of common law and statutory duties on the part of the perpetrators who acted recklessly and should have understood the risk of injury that their actions posed.

Again, a case such as this has serious implications for sport organizations. A new employee is like a new athlete. Both may know of hazing traditions and may expect to be initiated, even implicitly consenting. However, tradition, consent, or intent do not excuse others, including veteran athletes, coaches and administrators, from their legal responsibility to abide by the law in the initiation of new recruits.

ANTI-HAZING POLICIES

Anti-hazing policies have become somewhat commonplace in U.S. college and university Greek systems (sororities and fraternities). For example, the wording of the anti-hazing policy of Kappa Deuteron Chapter of Phi Gamma Delta International at the University of Georgia is typical of most Greek organizations (Phi Gamma Delta Web site). It reads as follows:

No chapter, colony, student or graduate Brother shall conduct nor condone hazing activities. Hazing activities are defined as: Any

action taken or situation created, intentionally, whether on or off fraternity premises, to produce mental or physical discomfort, embarrassment, harassment, or ridicule. Such activities may include but are not limited to the following: use of alcohol; paddling in any form; creation of excessive fatigue; physical and psychological shocks; quests, treasure hunts, scavenger hunts, road trips or any other such activities carried on outside or inside of the confines of the chapter house; wearing of public apparel which is conspicuous and not normally in good taste; engaging in public stunts and buffoonery; morally degrading or humiliating games and activities; and any other activities which are not consistent with academic achievement, fraternal law, ritual, or policy, or the regulations and policies of the educational institution, or applicable state law.
(www.uga.edu/fiji/nohazing.htm, retrieved December 23, 2002)

The website goes on to list the anti-hazing policy of the University of Georgia (which also applies to the athletic program), as well as the state of Georgia hazing statute.

Anti-hazing laws in athletics have been slower to materialize, yet are becoming more important to grade schools, junior high and high schools, and colleges and universities. Many states in the U.S. require educational institutions to develop anti-hazing policies (Rosner and Crow, 2002). Oftentimes school-wide anti-hazing policies are written to incorporate all school-sponsored organizations, including athletic teams, so no specific athletic anti-hazing policies are produced. Interestingly, Heather Findlay, a Canadian researcher, argues that hazing falls into the broader category of harassment, and as such can be included in an anti-harassment policy (1998). However, her research has shown several potential problems associated with policy development: (1) that each sport organization is unique and therefore any policy that governs it should be specific to the sport; and, (2) that sport has its own culture regarding harassment and hazing that must be taken into account during policy development (Findlay, 1998). Therefore, hazing and harassment must be addressed proactively, with clear definitions, solid consequences, and alternative initiation rites, before athletic anti-hazing policy development begins (Findlay, 1998). Findlay further notes that the training of personnel enlisted to enforce the policy, budgetary considerations, and characteristics of students subjected to the policy must be taken into consideration (Findlay, 1998).

ATHLETIC ANTI-HAZING POLICY

There are several components that must be included in an anti-hazing policy:

- Hazing and other forms of harassment must be clearly defined to educators, coaches, administrators, athletes, and trainers.
- Safe and confidential mechanisms for reporting hazing, whether done by teammates, coaches, or outsiders, must be developed and clearly communicated.
- Educators, administrators, coaches, trainers, and athletes must be trained how to respond when hazing is alleged, and this response must be consistent regardless of sport or personnel involved.
- Penalties must be clearly defined and consistently enforced.
- An anti-hazing workshop must be conducted, at the conclusion of which a student-athlete contract, stating understanding of the definition, penalties, and consequences of hazing, must be signed by each athlete on campus.
- Athletes' off-field behavior must be included in coaches' evaluation.
- A strong anti-hazing message must be publicized.
- Alternative team-building and initiation practices must be developed and implemented.

These basic components, or derivatives thereof, should be included in every athletic team's anti-hazing policy. Certainly this list can be expanded based on team-specific situations and in consultation with an experienced attorney. It is recommended that a program-wide meeting be held at the beginning of each academic year to discuss the policy and have each athlete sign it, acknowledging their consent to abide by its contents. Further, a team-specific meeting should be held at the beginning of each individual season to introduce new participants to returning players and familiarize them with the anti-hazing policy. This may also take place in a retreat-like setting where positive team-building and initiation rites can be performed.

SUMMARY

Hazing and other harassment issues have become important in athletics due to increased media exposure. With this exposure comes more scrutiny of how athletic department and school administrators can respond to and prevent hazing. This chapter has addressed the prevalence of hazing in athletics, ways in which victims may bring action against perpetrators and school districts, penalties, and consequences. Further, a model anti-hazing policy was proposed.

REFERENCES

ABC News. (2000). *Hazing.* Available at: abcnews.go.com/sections/us/Daily-News/hazing000828.html.

Crouch, E. (September 19, 1995). "Hazing law upheld." *Missouri digital news.* Available at: www.mdn.org/1995/stories/haze.htm.

Crow, R. (2001). "Hazing," in Cotton, Wolohan and Wilde (Eds.), *Law for recreation and sport managers* (2nd ed.). Kendall-Hunt: Dubuque, IA.

Crow, R. and Rosner, S. (2002). "Institutional and organizational liability for hazing in intercollegiate and professional team sports," *St. John's law review* 76(1): 87–114.

ESPN. (April 10–14, 2000). *Outside the lines—Hazing.* Available at: www.espn.go.com/otl/hazing/monday.html.

Findlay, H. (Summer 1998). "Harassment: What we are learning about what we are doing," *CAHPERD journal* 64(2): 32–34.

Hoover, N. (1999). *National survey: Initiation rites and athletics for NCAA sports teams.* Available at: www.alfred.edu/news/html/hazing_study.html.

MacMillan Bloedel Limited v IWA-Canada, Local 363. (1997). 50 C.L.A.S. (B.C.)

Nuwer, H. Available at: www.stophazing.org; www.hazing.hanknuwer.com/

Phi Delta Gamma. (2002). *Anti-hazing policy.* Available at: www.uga.edu/fiji/-nohazing.htm.

Rosner, S. and Crow, R. (2002). "Institutional liability for hazing in interscholastic sports," *Houston Law Review* 39(2): 276–300.

State Hazing Statutes

Alabama Hazing Law § 16-1-23.

Arizona Hazing Law 15-2301.

Arkansas Hazing Law § 6-5-201

California Hazing Law—Education Code Section 32050-32051

Colorado Hazing Law—Senate Bill 106 1999 Colo. SB 106

Delaware Hazing Law—§ 9301

Florida Hazing Law—240.1325

Georgia Hazing Law—§ 16-5-61

Idaho Hazing Law—Title 18, Chapter 9 Crimes and Punishment, Assault and Battery 18-917

Illinois Hazing Law—§ 720 ILCS 120/5

Kentucky Hazing Law—§ 164.375.

Louisiana Hazing Law—1801

Minnesota Hazing Law—127.465 Hazing policy

Missouri Hazing Law—§ 578.360–578.365

Nebraska Hazing Law—§ 28-311.06–28-311.07

New York Hazing Law—§ 120.16–120.17

North Carolina Hazing Law—14.35

Tennessee Hazing Law —49-7-123

Texas Hazing Law—Penal Code Section 4.52–4.58

Utah Hazing Law—§ 76-5-107.5

Vermont Hazing Law—NO. 120. An Act Relating to the Crime of Hazing S.76

Virginia Hazing Law—§ 18.2–56

Washington Hazing Law—§ 28B.10.900

CHAPTER 3

"No Mercy Shown Nor Asked"— Toughness Test or Torture?

Hazing in Military Combat Units and Its "Collateral Damage"

Gregory Malszecki
York University

Just think how the soldier is treated. While still a child he is shut up in the barracks.

During his training he is always being knocked about. If he makes the least mistake he is beaten, a burning blow on his body, another on his eye, perhaps his head is laid open with a wound. He is battered and bruised with flogging.
—Egyptian, ca. 1500 BCE

How seductive is war! When you know your quarrel to be just and your blood ready for combat, tears come to your eyes. The heart feels a sweet loyalty and pity to see one's friend expose his body … Alongside him, one prepares to live or die. From that comes a delectable sense which no one who has not experienced it will ever know. Do you think that a man who has experienced that can fear death? Never!
—Jean de Breuil, 15th century knight

For the young recruits, basic training is the closest thing their society can offer to a formal rite of passage, and the institution probably stands in an unbroken line of descent from the lengthy ordeals by which young males in precivilized groups were initiated into the adult community of warriors.
—Gwynne Dyer, contemporary military analyst

Despite democratization and the numerous open civic governments of the modern period, we still seem to desire secret societies, just as we have throughout recorded history and likely prehistory, where membership in cults, gangs, sects, social clubs, combat units, sports teams, fraternities, elite schools, and guilds often required "tests" of eligibility, initiation for membership status. The rituals and practices of secret societies have been overlooked by the broader historical and contemporary studies of human activity, though some specific manifestations have attracted attention in anthropology and, occasionally, in history, social science, and religious studies.

Hazing has aboriginal roots. The classic anthropological study of Arnold van Gennep (1960) on rites of passage rituals in early communities described initiations for individuals as marking major events or points of departure in a life cycle; rituals typically reflected transition from one status to another through stages of separation, transition, and incorporation. These stages may involve taboos of normal behaviour or reversals of it, or the creation of special bonds to the group through a set of trials or symbolic tasks to acquire knowledge or insight. On completion, the individual is fully recognized with new status in the group, all of whom have passed through similar ritual activities or ordeals. Membership can last for life or be limited to a certain time-period or set of contributions, but the affiliation usually requires some test of worth and desire as part of the rite of passage from outsider to insider.

Among the most ancient and important "insider" groups (besides prehistory religious mysteries societies) have been military societies, either warrior-cults of tribal peoples or large combat units in the armies of civilization. Gwynne Dyer characterizes the military group: "They have to be different, for their job is ultimately about killing and dying, and those things are not a natural vocation for any human being" (1985). Soldiers are trained to be professionals in warfare who have the same values no matter what group or unit they serve. But armies are made from men trained to fight alongside fellow soldiers with an intense sense of brotherhood and loyalty; soldiers identify with comrades in their unit. This group loyalty better guarantees safety, success, and survival in combat. The foundation for the loyal fighting unit must be made—not at the front or during the half-hour before combat begins—but in training when raw, usually young and impressionable, recruits are turned into a fighting unit. This initiation and training is achieved through discipline, enthusiasm, deprivation, and, in the end, restructured identity. If they submit and conform, they will wear the uniform with pride on the parade-ground; later, in combat, they may give up their lives in solidarity. Contempt for those failing basic training affirms the dignity of those who pass. An additional initiation for the combat unit is the unit's informal, often violent and distressing, initiation rituals. Similar brainwashing techniques and initiation works on sports teams, which, like the combat unit, demand loyalty and action for the "fighting" unit, though, as Dyer comments, "what sets soldiers apart is their willingness to kill" (1985: 103). People have to be trained to kill in a combat unit, trained to accept being killed. Quite deliberately, the military exploits strong cultural associations with the mythic heroes or heroic practices of its war-making society, while staying away from any focus on the distinct possibility of pain, injury, or death in the war zone. Instead, killing is associated with a higher purpose and with an enlarged vision of the self through identification with the ethos of the archetypal "warrior" and the code of honour. That code embodies a set of skills and warrior-values that helps gain victory in engagements through group cohesion.

McCarthy's (1994) socio-historical survey of warrior values finds time and time again a bond between warrior values and a society's conventional notions of masculinity. There are five main areas of bonding that young men especially find attractive: physical courage, endurance, strength, skill, and honour (especially evident as loyalty to leader and comrades without regard for personal risk). Failure to act, cowardice, or inability to endure pain shames men in such societies, not only the individual man, or the soldier, but also family and the greater community. There were warrior castes in the West right up through the nineteenth century, but the breakdown of the aristocracy, the erosion of elites through universal education and political franchise, the shift to cities and industrial production, the population explosion, the crisis of masculinity as a response to the feminist challenges for emancipation, and the bureaucratization of military command, began to dissolve the warrior values of old. But, ironically, in the very midst of the killing fields of World War One where machine guns cut down advancing lines at distances of 1,000 metres, and artillery blasted troops kilometres away, there was a renewal of the idealization of the manly warrior. From the terrible and protracted trench-warfare of the Great War came an intensification of the warrior values which encouraged individual heroism in the name of "comradeship, solidarity and mutual support of the small group, individual initiative and endurance" (McCarthy, 1994: 106). In the newly formed tactical special cadres, such as the Waffen-SS, British SAS, the U.S. Rangers and Navy Seals, and the Canadian Airborne, the *esprit de corps* of unit identification was a huge component of their training.

Characteristic of elite military forces everywhere, training in these new forces is more rigorous, the emphasis on symbolism higher. Their battle performance reflects better group cohesion and morale, especially in their decisive forcefulness in retaliating for any injury to one of their members— an example of how outsiders just do not count as much, even those on the same side but not the same unit. Recruits are initiated as new members of the "family"—an aggressive, tough, elite, highly skilled, and loyal combat team. Highly wrought and elaborate secret rituals imbue the entrant with a prescription for becoming a hero of the warrior culture in the security of group approval.

The English word "hero" is likely derived from an Indo-European proto-root meaning "he who keeps guard over." The designation is significant because of the primacy communities have placed on its heroes as those who give the gift of security through their willingness to give their own lives to protect the community (Gerzon, 1982). The boy who would become, or is called to become, a hero in combat, discovers through rites of passage and then warfare that the warrior-soldier chooses suffering without cowardice or crying, chooses to endure his own fears rather than surrender to them, chooses obedience to the group over his sense of self-preservation, and chooses death before dishonour or cowardice. The measure of worth in battle, the ultimate test, is the demonstration of courage in the face of terror; the strain and horror of war tempts most normal people with dereliction of duty and utter fear.

Since one cannot wait until hostilities break out to test future warrior-soldiers, armed forces and societies anticipating war must precondition youth. Motivating, testing, and affirming the untried is accomplished through both the rite of passage of punishing basic training and through initiations into the fighting unit. Hazing is presented as "games" that educate the initiate into the grammar of violence by playing out ritualized roles of submission and success. In hazing, the confusing mix of play and violence, pain and encouragement, fear and joy, ordeal and acceptance, and the hyper-exaggerated sense of brutality fuelled by the mental dis-orientation of alcohol-abuse (hazing is almost always accompanied by massive dosages of alcohol), works to prove that honourable loyalty to the group is the highest good; not life, not one's own life. In the midst of the danger and the aggression of hazing, participants separate from civilian or personal identity—farmer, clerk, student, and labourer—and become a fully functioning member of a fighting band of brothers. The initiation thus detaches the normal self from the ordinary individual, through the supposed ecstasy (literally, "out of one's self") and the magnificent feeling of liberation of the self, enabling full identification with the combat unit. Once initiated into the combat unit, "selfish" desires are submerged to attain the common goal; there is an energized group morale, connected to mythology, in which the power of union with others is deeper than normal mortal fear.

The hazing functions as a time-honoured consecration of loyalty among those who go against the norm by putting themselves in harm's way. J. Glenn Gray says that the soldier on the battlefield "is often sustained solely by the determination not to let down his comrades ... Men are true comrades only when each is ready to give up his life for the other, without reflection and without thought of personal loss" (1970: 47). This self-negation builds trust and reciprocal respect; adherents can deal with the predictable and terrible conditions of battle when the ultimate act is the very stuff of heroes—celebrated, though often unsung. Of course, there are also instances of hazing in the military that are devised by sociopaths or sadists who enjoy the pain and humiliation of others under the guise of "building" group cohesion through initiation. But, many soldiers report that hazing rites inspire and celebrate the mutual "love" between warrior-soldiers who are willing to die together and for each other in battle.

Through training and initiation, the soldier is made into a special kind of person, one who has learned to override all the biological and cultural prohibitions against killing a fellow human. In *On killing* (1996), Lt. Col. David Grossman argues that it is difficult to train people to kill one another, but that the mechanisms of doing so are well-understood and universally practiced wherever soldiers or police are required to use lethal force. A completely artificial process of sustained group approval is required to be successful in so severely altering identity that the greatest taboo can be violated without question and upon command. "Warriors cannot be like others, for having killed and escaped being killed; one can only feel an equal to those who know the terrible choices and temptations of cowardice in the midst of collective murder and conscripted brutality. Irrevocably, the killing floor of battle cuts [fighting] men off from women, children, and any others who have not learned the trade of warriors" (Malszecki, 1995: 2–3). The occupation of soldier requires a demonstration of power beyond ordinary human comfort and above ordinary human experience; it demands extraordinary suppression of fear and exceptional functioning under duress. The military objectives of a nation or a community could not be attained if the impulse to self-preservation as one of the deepest urges of humans could be not manipulated.

We could go to the Bible or the *Iliad* for a study of war as men's business, or for information on the training of soldiers or to the earliest myths and histories for explanations of the ethos of the battlefield, but little exists on hazing practices. There is some understanding about Spartan rituals, and the practices of Greek military clubs; we have the Roman *iuventus*, and military anecdotes and the documents on the medieval apprenticeship in arms with its sacramental induction into the order of knighthood. Records of hazing in military units begin to appear with greater frequency in the mid-nineteenth century, together with citations of abuse.

In the modern warfare of the nineteenth century the use of firearms and bombing had magnified the killing power of armies. As well, nation-states had been empire-building with the human resources of huge armies and navies of citizen-soldiers. Warfare was deadlier than ever, leading to a renewed urgent emphasis on male bonding for protection and assistance on the battlefield. Carl Sagan studies changes in the killing power of modern armies equipped with ever-new technology and mass recruiting. He finds that the killing power of modern weaponry increased by a billion-fold from the 1863 battle of Gettysburg in the American Civil War to the end of the Cold War in 1989, but that we are not a billion times wiser (Sagan, 1988). Under the pressures of rising death tolls unimaginable in earlier military hostilities, and as military leadership moves from warrior ethos to managerial bureaucracy, soldiers are left more on their own to seeking protection and security. Peers in the combat unit always had the greatest concern and the greatest stake in individual performance in combat, but become even more important with leadership at a greater distance. The "band of brothers in arms" becomes the prime determinant of an individual's fate on the killing ground. It makes sense then that these "brothers" would supervise the testing of worth and character of the "rookie" [the word itself derives from English slang for "recruit" from the French for "new growth"]. Toughness and the ability to suffer pain without complaint are prized; refusal to reveal the ordeal out of loyalty and affiliation is expected. Hazing continues in the hands of the lowly combat unit in the big, industrialized machine of modern warfare.

Grossman lists a soldier's key factors in the anatomy of killing: the demands of authority, group absolution, emotional distance, the nature of the victim, and the predisposition of the killer. These factors he claims are the root of the degree of death and destruction that made the twentieth century the bloodiest in human history. These factors also take modern armies of soldiers beyond the limits of human endurance in the sheer scale of war, leaving them highly vulnerable to post-traumatic stress disorders long past the end of conflict. Accountability to one's fellow soldiers in a battle unit combines with the anonymity of war to reduce personal responsibility—a soldier feels he will be letting his comrades down if he does not kill. The more powerful the psychological bond with the group, the more legitimate the demand for killing will be if group members are close by. When Audie Murphy, "the most decorated American soldier of World War II," was asked what motivated him to take on a German infantry company by himself and capture more than one hundred, he replied, "They were killing my friends" (Grossman, 1996: 151).

A soldier's environment is regulated and artificially arranged to an extent civilians can only compare in terms of very strict schooling or imprisonment. The shared training, the uniforms, the new status, and the brotherhood of arms cultivated by the armed forces themselves increase the allure of informal initiations at the unit level, and suggest that research needs to be done on whether hazing is altering in severity as a response to the newly emerging battlefield conditions, the machine-human interface of the new weaponry, and the remote managerial direction of the command staff and officer corps. The prime task of commanders "has been to bring soldiers to the field of battle" (Bercuson, 1996). By strengthening the "in-group/out-group" mentality through the rites of passage, the unit will be predictably more aggressive in eliminating adversaries in fighting, but also more easily identified through the actions of any of its members. There is also a predictable increase in mutual support for peers as well as increased hostility in retaliation for injury or death caused to one of its members. The intensification of both positive and negative emotions compressed in the same way in all the group participants will enable the group to function more reliably under fire and in attaining military objectives. So battle (or its likelihood) produces a sense of the sublime in the love soldiers have for those close to them who share the same fate. But things can go "renegade" in the exercise fighting group veterans with unchallengeable power initiating the rookies, and the abuses deserve a closer look.

Let us look at the recent prohibitions against hazing in military units and reflect on their appearance as a response to public revelations and the public's subsequent revulsion rather than a genuine assertion of command over renegade practices. In the Canadian, American, and Russian armed forces, there was public outrage expressed when evidence surfaced of bizarre, sadistic, and protracted forms of torture and bullying as initiations that sometimes resulted in death and severe injuries. Bercuson (1996) claims that the two hidden video recordings of the Airborne Division sealed its fate and forced the federal government to disband it with dishonour. When American national television broadcast the pain and humiliation of tortured novices, and the glee and sadism of the veterans, American Marines had to defend themselves against charges of brutality, charges made with the public's blessing. However, nothing was said about the secret video-taping of the "blood pinning rituals" for completing ten successful parachute jumps. The death of a Russian soldier unleashed a furious condemnation when the world press detailed the abuse of large numbers of conscripts. Although the senior command everywhere responded with absolute prohibition and claims of ignorance, their implementation of new policies did very little to eliminate the hazing at the unit levels. Unofficial leaks from the ranks suggested that hazing is frequent; clearly, traditions have much more hold on the current practices than the military leadership does. Particularly disturbing is the collision between today's integration of females into combat units and the misogynist rituals in previously all-male units. The testing of recruits is done by the very comrades one is dependent on for safety and protection. The incidents at the military academies in the United States, not just West Point and the Air Force Academy, but the Citadel and the Virginia Military Institute as well, confirm that women soldiers experience duress beyond the torturous bullying that is the "norm" for males, often with the covert support of many officers who resist integration of females into combat units. But how stable have "norms" been even for males? This may never be known, since most participants are sworn to a secrecy that is maintained for life, and also because intensity of initiations vary a great deal in different military communities.

According to the *Oxford English dictionary*, there has been a solid set of known traditions surrounding obnoxious and bullying hazing in universities and in the armed forces since the middle of the nineteenth century (*OED,* online). This brutal behaviour has been safeguarded by threats to anyone disclosing the rituals to authorities or the public; the silence is palpable. Do modern practices of hazing offer us any insight into the perpetuation of such secret initiations? A public discussion is emerging on deeply-held concerns about the validity of rationales for the hazing in the military; there are rejections of hazing and alternatives available for producing positive results for group cohesion in schools, fraternities, sport teams, or combat units. Nevertheless, military combat, as always, is an environment of extreme. Under such circumstances, there is special concern for the protection of rituals that promote the sacrifice for comrades, necessary in combat, and demonstrated when it comes to hazing. An Israeli soldier comments,

> Fighting is a social art, based upon collective activity, cooperation and mutual support ... this utter reliance on others is an integral part of the effort to meet the enemy irrespective of odds, and it largely determines men's willingness to risk their lives in pressing the attack ... In short there is rarely brotherhood in facing death when there is none in peace. (Dyer, 1985: 105)

There are many examples of tribal cultures that withhold the claim of manhood from adolescent males until they have successfully completed a coming-of-age ritual, but in modern industrialized societies the institutional equivalent of man-making through hazing or ritual is most evident in the military. Although street gangs and college team sports have devised their own rituals, and the stakes can be very high, especially for desperate, impoverished street youth, the military requires extraordinary action and attitudes of complete faith and loyalty to fellow-soldiers. As Lynne Segal analyzes in *Slow motion: Changing masculinities, changing men,* "the friendships and extreme male bonding of men [in the military] can, ironically, evoke the intense emotional compassion, self-sacrifice, love and devotion associated more with 'femininity.' These emotions have no parallel in the restrained, self-sufficient 'masculinity' thought appropriate for men in civilian life" (1990). The "insider-outsider" separation also serves as a buffer against the pain and guilt of killing in war. Amidst the physical risks of death and maiming, the fatigue, anxiety, emotional exhaustion, and terror, as well as the possible risk of becoming a psychiatric casualty, the combat group offers a measure of accountability but also the very real benefits of anonymity and group absolution for the act of killing. As Konrad Lorenz put it, "man is not a killer, but the group is" (Grossman, 1996: 151).

Training exercises for the modern soldier-recruit are planned to be as realistic as possible, physically demanding, and even risky, but the trainees are not at war and this often incites disciplinary problems. Bercuson describes young and spirited soldiers who would need discipline in any institution (1996). He says that restless soldiers sometimes look for ways to undermine authority or test the limits of possible behaviour. They are looking for tests and rituals among themselves. He concludes that

> the invention of bizarre rituals and initiation rites to test their mettle and manhood is not uncommon. In battle, there is no room for such artificial rites of passage. The only rite of passage that matters in war is that which a soldier endures when the enemy tries to kill him [or a member of his unit]. (1996: 139)

Certainly not every unit in the armed forces develops its "group chemistry" the same way, not even among the elite Special Forces. In Canada, the elite Airborne was disbanded for the excesses, including hazing, but also for the crimes and abuses of some members. The unit are characterized as having a "biker-gang mentality" in Bercuson's *Significant incident: Canada's army, the Airborne, and the murder in Somalia.* Some thugs in this unit directly challenged the authority of the chain of command with a series of troublesome offences and disciplinary problems. Non-commissioned officers trying to deal with enlisted anti-social soldiers were not effectively supported by commanders. Bercuson carefully analyzes the failed attempts to cope with the so-called "bad apples." He illustrates that solutions were slowed by career decisions and neglect by higher command, and also hampered by inadequate federal financing of the armed forces.

Bercuson recounts:

> A vicious streak of racism and anti-social behaviour ran through the
> regiment, particularly No. 2 Commandos. Degrading hazing rituals
> for new recruits, some of which involved not only verbal but also
> physical abuse and degradation (such as being forced to eat feces),
> had become the norm. On July 30 [1992], and again on August 30,
> some of these hazings were carried out behind the barracks of No. 2
> Commando. On the second occasion, a captain from the regimental
> HQ was present with some forty-nine master corporals and corporals.
> Videotapes of portions of such hazings would show up later on
> CBC-TV. (1996: 215–216)

When the repugnant initiations were shown on television early in 1995
following the investigation of the murder of a Somalian youth by Airborne peacekeepers, the public disgust and political embarrassment
resulted in the order for disbandment on January 23, 1995, by Minister of
National Defense, David Collenette. Any core values of dedicated honour
and combat-readiness in this unit were subverted by political and bureau-
cratic fall-out, but the videos of hazing and abuses also seemed to
demonstrate none of the virtues of small-group bonding essential for
battle-effectiveness or bonding. What the public witnessed were a secret
series of "freak show" sadomasochistic power-plays where rookies were
victimized for the pleasure and privilege of the veteran masters of ceremonies and assembled Airborne spectators. Other military abuses surfaced
in the same way elsewhere, with similar public revulsion and prompt official
prohibitions from top-level commanders despite resistance in the ranks.

In 1991 and 1993, video clips of "blood-pinning" incidents—where
U.S. Marine paratroopers who had completed ten training paratroop
jumps were subjected to painful pounding of the pins into the chests of
the rookies until blood was drawn—were taken, and later shown on
national TV. In 1997, Defense Secretary William Cohen, claiming he was
"disturbed and disgusted" by the footage, also cited about eighty hazing
incidents in the Marine Corps in the previous three to five years (*Houston
chronicle*, 1997). A Marine investigation in a 1993 report stated that the
real problem is "a systematic one," finding that at one base alone Marines
were punched, kicked, forced to swallow lighted cigarettes, and smeared

with excrement. The Marine Commandant ordered unit commanders to see that the practice was halted, but others, including a vice-admiral for a Washington defense watchdog group, predicted that "zero tolerance of such practices would be a tough goal to meet." In his words, "You can put out all kinds of rules and regulations. The problem with hazing is you don't discover it until it has taken place." Even though Marine Corps officials stated that fifty-two Marines had been court-martialed between 1994 and 1997 for taking part in hazing, and that another thirty-four received non-judicial punishment including dishonourable discharges, there was still a defensiveness on the part of units who see this as an ordeal preparatory to combat. One officer said, "What's a couple of pin pricks? It could be an AK-47. Yeah, blood pinning is terrible, but war is terrible" (*Houston chronicle*, 1997).

The Marine Corps Order 1700.28 of June 18, 1997, on the subject of hazing, cites as background that this is a leadership issue and a military issue:

> Marines do not go into harm's way, make the sacrifices they always have, or give up their precious lives because they have been hazed or initiated into some self-defined, "elite" subculture. They perform these heroic acts of selflessness because they are United States Marines and because they refuse to let their fellow Marines down. (Marine Corps Office, 1997)

The order goes on to emphasize that every Marine will treat every other Marine with respect and dignity, then it promotes ceremonies and social events that "serve to enhance morale, esprit de corps, pride, professionalism, and unit cohesiveness. Unfortunately, some in our ranks confuse hazing with the tradition of certain military ceremonies and develop initiations or 'rites of passage' they believe promote loyalty. They do not" (1997). Hazing is given an extensive and detailed definition; they clearly elaborate on the policy statement that "Hazing is prohibited," outlining the actions to be taken for infractions. However, six months after that very order forbidding hazing from the Marine Corps Commandant, a twenty-year-old private lost his spleen among other injuries as part of a beating that landed four other Marines in jail on charges of hazing. The more senior trainees were bullying the newer ones in fights called "love sessions" but those refusing to fight had their heads flushed in toilets; there were further allegations of mock crucifixions taping broomsticks to hands through the backs of trainee shirts (Smith, 1998).

These surfacing military scandals have revealed the poor credibility of official policies, especially when more and more survivors of abusive behaviour testify about ongoing practices, and also, collusion, on the part of mid-level and senior level commanders. This is not to mention the "counseling" received in the ranks regarding voicing concerns or intentions to become whistleblowers. Prominent among the cases is also the emergence of traditions of cruel bullying consecrated at military academies such as West Point or the U.S. Air Force Academy. The entrance of female recruits into the armed forces and military academies has provided abundant evidence of the traditional militarized "masculinity" that is often emphasized through hazing, which some evidence indicates as particularly intense when female initiates are subjected to the rituals. The cases at the Virginia Military Academy and the Citadel highlight a problem that has accompanied the introduction of women into combat units. The simulated rape as part of POW training fictionalized in the film *G.I. Jane* (where the Demi Moore character successfully undergoes the brutal Navy Seal training as the lone female) actually happens in real-life incidents in the military. There is the Canadian example of the scandal of "interrogation training" of a female officer or the Air Force Academy example where thirty cadets (including at least one female) watched without intervening as a female cadet was beaten unconscious three times and subjected to "simulated rape." No one was held accountable in the Honour Board finding. Even though hazing rites of passage are rooted in the male traditions of the warrior, there is little to suggest that females entering the armed forces are refusing to engage in the practices, although there is protest about the excesses and brutality. When the West Point hazing scandal of 1898–1901 broke into the public press, Mark Twain wrote that "the men who indulge in hazing are bullies and cowards" (*Stophazing*, 2003). But women recruits will go along. The singular dedication for both male and female soldiers to a masculine definition of the heroic warrior clearly forces female recruits to meet the tests as "warriors" not as females.

Hazing is presented in the military as a practice that accompanied the formation of warriors long before the organization of the first civilized armies, long into our recorded past. Chief reasons for such ritual are to separate the warrior-recruit from a civilian identity, and to encourage bonds with the members of the combat unit. Hazing is also a term that has had a long association with beatings and thrashings, brutal horseplay, and cruel harassment by veterans or officers for newcomers. The *Oxford English dictionary* provides records of the custom in both nautical (1840, "let an officer once say 'I'll haze you' and your fate is fixed") and collegial settings (1860 [*Harvard Magazine*], "The absurd and barbarous custom of hazing, which has long prevailed in the college"). One 1868 entry records that upper year bullies had "gagged his mouth … shaved his head, then put him under the pump, and left him tied on the campus" (*OED*, online). There is a reference to a death at Yale in 1892: "'Hazing' at Yale has unhappily led to the death of an unfortunate young student named Rustin, and to a general denunciation of this custom as 'stupid and brutal.'" All OED mentions of "hazing" link this behaviour to beating, harassment, bullying, and to cruel horseplay intended to frighten or scold or punish with blows as an exercise of power under the guise of "toughening up" the newcomer.

There is good reason to recognize that increasing lethality on the battlefield throughout the twentieth century, together with more and more remote chains of command in military bureaucracies, resulted in pressure on the smallest combat units to "proof" its members themselves, ostensibly to encourage group loyalty by tying the recruit's emotional bonds to the unit, a sensible adaptation in the face of mechanized combat and group survival; however, we also find that hazing abuse exceeds the rationale for group cohesion. The military academies can no longer pretend that these excessive hidden rituals and secret cruelties are necessary for building unit loyalty and honourable endurance.

The last point in this chapter identifies the link between combat teams and sports teams; the majority of instances of hazing in civilian communities are in sports team initiations. Recent scholars have studied the seduction of boys into a military mentality through the "hardening" promised by success in sports where surrogate fathers and older "veterans" would ensure that boys and young men could get the benefit of morale training in games as well as strength, skill, and conditioning. In this setting, young boys have to be repeatedly made to feel shame about their feelings, about any tendency to lose control and cry, about their lack of discipline which should keep feelings of vulnerability and fear in check. Sports came to be seen as a guarantee that the "manly traits" would be developed when the fun of games was tied to the rule-bound struggle for victory on the playing fields. For example, competitive games were the training-ground of aggressive class privilege among the British elite of the British Empire in the team sports of nineteenth-century public schools under innovators like Master Thomas Arnold at Rugby School in 1828. The more combative the sports, the less likely the charge of "sissy" (that is, derived from "sister") as ridicule on any boy who might be accused of not acting tough enough. This deliberate involvement of boys into sporting culture was selected as preconditioning for battle in the school system by authorities in England and its former colonies, including the United States. Masculine values were of extreme importance to the Empire, to nation-building, to success in management and business, and to the military. The so-called "crisis of masculinity" happened as a response to first wave feminism and the influence of the female in schools; the "crisis" engendered movements like the Boy Scouts and the YMCA as well as youth sport and the Playground Movement to re-instill masculine values in boys.

In *Manliness and militarism: Educating young boys in Ontario for war* (2001), Mark Moss details how sports were promoted for boys in Ontario during the early 1900s: "John Hobson, an influential early twentieth-century critic of imperialism, [who] recognized that the objective of sports and clubs was to mould young boys into men with the instincts of warriors" (122). The coaches for these adversarial sports contests came more and more to adapt the planning, strategy, and tactics of battle commanders, intentionally developing the abilities and skills suitable for combat, and often with the wholesale adoption of language from the military for sports terms (Malszecki, 1995).

Many contemporary scholars of gender history and sport sociology have identified the connections between sport and war, in particular, militarized masculinity, one that requires "toughening up" boys and young men into potential young soldiers:

> Cultures produce male warriors by toughening up boys from an early age … they are not innately "tougher" than girls. They do not have fewer emotions or attachments, or feel less pain. It is obvious from the huge effort that most cultures make to mold "tough" boys that this is not an easy or natural task. (Goldstein, 2001)

Canadian Michael Smith's *Violence and sport* (1988) and the current studies by sport and gender sociologists Michael Messner and Don Sabo in the United States are among those that have addressed the equation of sport and war. The "rhetoric of toughness" is detailed in Myriam Miedzian's chapter on militaristic coaching (1991). This scholarship examines how a romanticization of war and the values of war have been absorbed by competitive athletics at every level, both kids and professionals. Initiations, or hazing among team sports, especially in college sport, among both male and female teams, become part of the "war" package for sport.

In this chapter we have seen that military training has long enjoyed success in transforming civilian adolescents into soldiers by providing training in lethal skills and initiation into group identity. The tradition of testing the mettle of recruits before the moment of armed conflict is probably a part of our prehistory as much as it is part of our recorded history. In recent times, the increasing mechanization of the modern battlefield and the complexity and bureaucratization of military management have put pressure on the smaller combat units to use hazing to elicit the requisite "team chemistry" and group cohesion. As well, there are understandable reasons for the seriousness and severity of the hazing in the military—the specialized work of soldiers, unlike that of any other occupation, is about killing and dying. It is arguable that there is an increase in abusive hazing in elite, hard-core soldier units because of the magnified lethality of modern battle zones, but that the purposes of degrading and humiliating as well as hurting the recruits as a "test" of worth and trust have not changed appreciably throughout history. The combat team has received traditions and elaborated on them according to perceptions about survivability in battle. In the higher-risk elite cadres such as the Canadian Airborne or the U.S. Marines, the rite of passage is viewed with even more intensity. The gender integration of the past couple of decades in both combat teams and military academies reflects the extent and cruelty of the traditions, especially if female recruits suffer additional cruelties. Excesses work against desired combat cohesiveness.

The cultural connections of war and modern sport show a clear, mutual link to the preparation of young men for a potential turn of duty in war. The common ground between the military and sport team hazing needs more complete study, especially in light of recent scholarship prompted by societal disapproval of bullying as anti-social behaviour. Military hazing is very much part of the problem of war-making. Hazing in schools and sports is a problem of aggressive and violent tendencies even in communities in peacetime. If hazing is seen as bullying or even torture and criminal behaviour, can we eliminate these rites of passage? Long-held expectations that such ceremonies "build" necessary warrior-soldiers must be examined and understood in order to remove abuses. The Charter for UNESCO has indicated that the battle for nurturing hearts and minds must be won both in society and the armed forces simultaneously: "That since wars begin in the minds of men, it is in the minds of men that that the defenses of peace must be constructed" (Constitution, 1945, www.icomos.org).

REFERENCES

Bercuson, D. (1996). *Significant incident: Canada's army, the Airborne, and murder in Somalia*. Toronto: McClelland and Stewart.

Constitution of the United Nations Educational, Scientific, and Cultural Organization. (1945). Available at: www.icomos.org/unesco_constitution.html.

Davies, M. (2002). *Introducing anthropology*. Toronto: Penguin Books.

Dyer, G. (1985). *WAR*. Toronto: Stoddart.

Gennep, Arnold van. (1960). *The rites of passage*. Monika B. Vizedom and Gabrielle L. Caffe, trans. Chicago: University of Chicago Press.

Gerzon, M. (1982). *A choice of heroes: The changing faces of American manhood*. Toronto: Houghton Mifflin.

Gilmore, D. (1990). *Manhood in the making: Cultural concepts of masculinity*. New Haven: Yale University Press.

Goldstein, J. (2001). *War and gender: How gender shapes the war system and vice versa*. Cambridge: Cambridge University Press.

Gray, C. (1997). *Postmodern war: The new politics of conflict*. New York: The Guilford Press.

Gray, J. (1970). *The warriors: Reflections on men in battle*. New York: Harper.

Grossman, D. (1996). *On killing: The psychological cost of learning to kill in war and society*. Toronto: Little, Brown and Company.

Houston Chronicle News Services. (1997). "Cohen rips 'blood pinning' and other military hazing." Available at: www.chron.com/content/chronicle/page1/97/02/01/military.html.

Malszecki, G. (1995). *"He shoots! He scores!": Metaphors of war in sport and the political linguistics of virility*. Unpublished doctoral dissertation. York University, Toronto.

Marine Corps Order 1700.28. (18 June 1997). *Marine Corps policy on hazing.* Marine Corps Commandant Charles Krulak. Available at: www.tecom.usmc.mil/ utm/MCO%201700.28.htm

McCarthy, B. (1994). "Warrior values: A socio-historical survey," in J. Archer (Ed.), *Male violence.* London: Routledge.

Miedzian, M. (1991). *Boys will be boys: Breaking the link between masculinity and violence.* New York: Anchor.

Moss, M. (2001). *Manliness and militarism: Educating young boys in Ontario for war.* Toronto: Oxford University Press.

Nuwer, H. (2003). [Review of the book *Bullies and cowards: The West Point hazing scandal: 1898–1901*]. Available at: www.stophazing.org/military/bulliesand cowards.htm

Oxford English Dictionary Online. (2003). Available at: http://dictionary.oed.com/cgi

Sagan, Carl. (1988). *Billions and billions: Thoughts on life and death at the brink of the millennium.* Thorndike, MN: Thorndike Press.

Segal, L. (1990). *Slow motion: Changing masculinities, changing men.* New Brunswick, N.J.: Rutgers University Press.

Smith, B. (1998). "Four marines charged in new round of hazing incidents." Available at: www.bergen.com/morenews/marine199802135.htm

Smith, M. (1988). *Violence and sport.* Toronto: Canadian Scholars' Press.

CHAPTER 4

A Search for a Theoretical Understanding of Hazing Practices in Athletics

Margery Holman

"Power issues are the base of all interactions, whether they be personal or professional. In turn, how one comes to define power and who is seen as having it affects those interactions" (Perry et al., 1992: 149). Associated with power and the exercise of power is the potential for abuse and violence. This chapter (i) explores how the power relationships in athletics are regularly reconstructed through the traditional practices of hazing and how these can be viewed as an act of violence and, (ii) provides an introduction to the ways in which hazing and power might intersect with gender. Many of the examples used are extracted from a larger study on harassment (Holman, 1995) within which hazing emerged as an issue of discussion.

HAZING, VIOLENCE, AND POWER

Hazing is an event created, historically, for a purpose. Athletic hazing has been defended as a means of creating team cohesion, believed to be an element critical to team success (Bryshun and Young, 1999; Hoffer, 1999; Sanday, 1990). However, there are many other ways in which team cohesion can be successfully achieved. This might then suggest that there are other purposes associated with the practice of hazing. One of these purposes is that hazing represents hierarchy and social dominance. These characteristics are symbolic of social and professional relationships outside the structure of an athletic team environment, relationships essential to capitalist patriarchy.

The contention that violence is reflected in hazing practices relies on a definition of violence that differs from the typical, day-to-day definitions. According to Ramazanoglu (1987), "violence should be understood as any action or structure that diminishes another human being" (64). When we accept this definition, we must acknowledge that the hazing actions that strip another individual of their freedoms, dignity, and self-identity, are components of a violent concept.

Historically, athletics has represented a hierarchy in which deference to male authority and sacrifice of individualism is commonplace. Athletic hazing is a system of control whereby rookie athletes defer to veterans and, in the process, acknowledge and confirm the veterans as the holders of power. Failure to support this relationship will threaten acceptance for group membership. The endorsement of hazing within the institution of athletics serves to emphasize power and hierarchy, both inherent characteristics in the veteran-rookie relationship. Status is earned through affiliation with a team, giving those with years of experience greater power and privilege. Through such structuring, Ramazanoglu (1987) notes that "[w]e must recognize the violence built into many of our institutions such as our schools and places of work in that they are competitive, hierarchical, non-democratic and at times unjust" (64). Techniques of subordination, which convey a message that violence can take a variety of forms, are employed to secure existing power structures. Hazing serves as one of these techniques. The diminishing of other human beings through the use of insults, inferiorizing, and subservience is a form of intimidation that coerces others to accept the autocracy and inequality of the structure, in this case, of sport. While establishing subordinate roles, veterans are able to assume dominant roles, characterized by a sense of being more important than those around them. The nature of this interaction, through the practice of hazing, serves as a social control that has been constructed for the purpose of educating members, immediately upon arrival, to the terms of their membership in the group.

Annual hazing rituals create a cycle whereby initiates (the hazed) eventually become the veterans (the hazers). This process re-establishes the team hierarchies at the beginning of each season. The extended lesson learned simultaneously is that power bestows permission to use that power at will. Hazing practices represent an abuse of power for the reconstruction and maintenance of advantageous power relations. The importance of protecting the right of veteran athletes to initiate the new inductees precludes any effort, in defense of the rights of the initiated, to terminate initiation practices. A university student, formerly a participant in Ontario's junior hockey system, noted that his first two experiences with hazing took place at the coach's house and the club president's house respectively (*Fifth estate*, 1997). A coach and a club president have a vested interest in the communication of control systems and use the veteran players to help achieve this control. Further, the use of power to control others in athletics parallels the expression of violence in society at large when power, regardless of its source, is used to control those who are devoid of such power.

So who are these social power brokers? Initiation has traditionally been an exercise engaged in by fraternities, the military and athletics (Nuwer, 1990: 1999). Most individuals have heard stories about the ways in which athletes are initiated as members of a team. Shaving the heads, eyebrows, or other body parts of rookies, painting their faces or other parts of the body, forced drinking of a large amount of alcohol, being forced to perform embarrassing, repulsive, or cruel games, and participating in humiliating or indecent conduct are some of the practices athletes have identified. One athlete suggested that "the alcohol was supposed to make me not care of what was going to happen" (Justin, personal communication, November, 1997).

Sport is a strong representation of patriarchy, where males dominate in every meaningful aspect and females are placed on the margins (Messner, 1992; Sabo, 1987). However, this gendered dichotomy is only a small piece of the hierarchy. Through sport, males learn that power is well defined. For example, coaches have it and players do not; athletes have it and non-athletes do not; seniors have it and others do not; males have it and females do not. Power gives people the right to do as they please, to expect privilege that is not readily available to others. It is important to exert this power over others so they, too, may learn the chain of command and learn how to assume the power when their turn comes.

When teams decide to initiate rookies, this chain of command is, in fact, what they are teaching. Rookies are stripped of their identity and forced to submit to the wishes of senior members of the team. Male athletes recount that they were required to strip and parade publicly in their jock straps, attend a party for a short time wearing only a party hat, and wear diapers. This submission is viewed as a means of creating solidarity that is considered essential to the success of the team. For new recruits, who so desperately want to belong to this group and to be accepted by veterans whom they in many cases have grown to admire, the power differential mandates their participation in hazing ritual. It is a process that results in individuals believing that it is a privilege to be a member of this special group and that the special attention is an honour for which to be grateful. In contrast, one university athlete noted, "many people think the players have choice .[whether to participate or not]. They do not" (Justin, personal communication, November 1997). The humiliation and isolation that they would experience by refusing to participate would be more intense and enduring than the humiliation experienced in an initiation ritual. Resistance is minimized by the ever-present threat of greater degradation. The power imbalance has orchestrated the perception that rookies want to be initiated and freely choose to be initiated in such a way that most, themselves, believe that they want to be initiated. It is believed that experiencing initiation is the only way to be accepted, to be successful on the team. On the other hand, avoiding initiation would be a cowardly act, and a rejection of the group and its principles of unity and power.

Sport has served as a training ground for boys to become men. In the process, men learn to control each other according to the hierarchies that have become tradition (Messner, 1992; Sabo, 1987; Whitson, 1990). This hierarchy, partly maintained through hazing, is one that emphasizes a superior–inferior dichotomy. Rookies, as inferior, must experience hazing to become accepted into manhood. They must show courage in the face of adversity. This is displayed in hazing events such as "the puck drop": "The basics of this event was a tied string around the player's genitals while a pail hung over a beam. Pucks were dropped one by one until the player could no longer withstand the pain. Each rookie took their turn and points were recorded for an ultimate humiliation that was to take place at the end of the night" (Justin, personal communication, November, 1997). Other events cited were the marshmallow game and push-ups. The marshmallow game involves placing a marshmallow in the rectum and running a prescribed path, then dropping the marshmallow in a cup, without any aids, at the end of the run. Failure to achieve this goal requires that the initiate eat the marshmallow. The push-ups referred to are done over a cup of beer for one minute; the initiate gets a point every time he successfully dunks his genitals in the beer (Justin, personal communication, November 1997). These events lack dignity according to common social standards. The initiates' willingness to acquiesce demonstrates the power of incumbents and of the system within which they operate.

HAZING, GENDER, AND POWER

Hazing rituals have no singular purpose and no singular outcome. As the context changes in sport hazing, the diversity of purpose and outcome expands. Experiences and the meanings attached to them vary depending upon the individuals and the environment involved. For example, males and females may recount a difference in experiences, which may be further exaggerated based upon a single-sex or coed setting. Similarly, the rituals attached to different sports, e.g., jockey vs. swimmer, may produce different outcomes. The discussion that follows introduces a gendered analysis of hazing in sport in an attempt to further understand the meanings that underlie sport hazing rituals and how they may contribute to excluding females and other marginalized groups from fully participating in sport as equals.

Misogyny carries a message that categorizes gender oppositionally, segregating women from men and maneuvering to deny status to women. Linked closely with the dimension of status, subordination through hazing is the interrelationship of gender with class. This interaction of power and gender is part of a social system. Robinson (1997) provides insight into the oppositional categories of gender with the following analysis: "Somehow, by humiliating and degrading a man and stripping him of his humanity, he becomes less than a man. The only people who aren't men in this world are women, and ... someone's got to take that role in a man's world where women don't exist" (79). She further notes that "the initiation purges soldiers and athletes of any femininity that dares to exist in them" (ibid.). While much of Robinson's quotation refers to the military, the concept can be applied to sport as well. Sport, historically, has been the domain of men, a social site for the development of masculinity.

Hazing contributes to the social reproduction of masculinity and femininity. First, the ritual itself is a carryover from male traditions and male-centered sport, and suggests "toughing it out" amongst male peers. Courage and ability to endure pain have always been integral parts of the initiation process. These characteristics serve as an important way in which to set males apart from females and to express males' superior ability and character. Surviving culminates in a solidarity among men that enables them to dominate those who are excluded from any access to this experience, women.

Within athletics, hazing practices have been most closely linked, at least publicly, with football and ice hockey (*Fifth estate*, 1997; Mandal, 1997; Robinson, 1998). Perhaps because of the influence of the military and of the media attention given to fraternities, hazing in sport has typically been associated with all-male settings. This does not, however, prevent other sports, including female teams, from engaging in hazing practices. In fact, a 1999 study by Alfred University provides evidence that hazing affects more than simply a couple of sports; this study also suggests that hazing exists on female teams. Most recently, the *Windsor star* newspaper (2003) reported on a Chicago high school powder puff football game and the violent hazing that accompanied the game.

In searching for the meaning behind initiations, we might make a link between the exclusiveness that the group communicates towards non-members and the dichotomous thinking that lends itself to dominant-subordinate relationships. Hazing becomes a necessity to demonstrate that, having survived the rigors of the ritual, an individual has gained the elevated social status of being a team member.

Men have traditionally maintained an exclusive hold on the domain of sport, especially important sport (CIAU, 1992; NCAA, 2002; Women's Sport Foundation, 1997). In the process of doing this, they have assigned women to their "appropriate" roles: generally secondary, non-decision-making positions. On occasion, the media expose their role as sexual objects available for the sexual gratification of males (King, 2003). Through these practices, women are often marginalized from sport per se and accepted only on male terms and in roles that men do not want. This sexualization and sexual division are often expressed in the social behaviours engaged in during hazing's male bonding and unification practices. These behaviours define inclusivity (being an accepted member of the group) and exclusivity (not being an accepted member of the group). Rookies have been told to wear women's clothing and to hire strippers for the gratification of veterans. These examples represent a gendered hierarchy. It would not be humiliating to dress as a woman if women were held in high regard and considered equals. Nor would it be acceptable to contract strippers if women were not sexualized for the purpose of servicing male sexual fantasy. Clearly the strong male presence with the use of a female presence to emphasize masculinity contributes to the message of sport as a sanctum for male privilege and control.

In hazing, where women are typically denigrated, exploited or made invisible, the status of females as secondary to males can be the meaning that is taught to both females and males. The structure of hazing can be a mechanism that teaches females, and again males, about the hierarchical scheme. A difference emerges because of the female location in the gender order, which emphasizes that there are restrictions on their ability to match the achievements of their higher-status male counterparts (Sabo and Panepinto, 1990). Hazing serves as a mechanism by which those with power and status educate others and ensure that they conform to the rules of the system.

Many behaviours engaged in during hazing within male-female combined sports would, under different circumstances, be considered sexual harassment. Practices such as being required to lick whipped cream and eat a cherry off the stomach of a teammate of the opposite sex, to eat a banana from the crotch of a male athlete, or to obtain signatures on breasts and buttocks all have sexual overtones that may well be offensive to those who are expected to engage in them. The sexual objectification of women is often built into hazing ritual, with and without female participation. This contributes to the continued oppression of women in both sport and society at large. Females learn to identify with a position of inferiority.

The growth of women's sport and the increased opportunity for females as participants should offer the possibility for change. However, women's programs and their associated roles and responsibilities have emulated a male model. The process has been two-pronged. Women have adopted practices, such as hazing, that have traditionally marginalized them. Their attempts to assimilate in a structure that works very hard at excluding them negate the potential transformation of sport. Secondly, in an attempt to be accepted as equals in a male world, they disassociate from the female 'other' or non-athletes whom they see as targets of male sexualization. Female athletes detail the following behaviours: placing a banana with whipped cream between the legs of a male athlete, and then licking the whipped cream and eating the banana; having males write on the bodies of female athletes, indirectly inviting these men to engage in sexually invasive activities; dressing up like sluts, in sexually degrading ways or in suggestive clothing; and doing push-ups over guys in their underwear. Female athletes engaging in self-oppression, as reflected in these behaviours, is a means by which male superiority is maintained. It reinforces the power structure that holds men dominant over women. When adopting the values and practices of males, females become active participants in their own sexualization and oppression. Females can never achieve equality by sacrificing their identity and making an effort to assume the identity that males want of them. Nor can they achieve equality by adopting the values of males while males fail to compromise or acknowledge their contribution to the social construction of gender and the hierarchies of power that oppress women.

In addition to marginalizing women, hazing practices are used to subordinate and marginalize homosexual males. Thus the practice of hazing not only elevates the status of masculinity, but also confirms the domination of heterosexual masculinity. Demanding that rookies visit a gay bar or dress up as gay is intended to be humiliate rookies, to strip them of their masculinity, and to make them feel less adequate as males than their veteran sponsors. These practices also validate heterosexual masculinity while censuring homosexuality.

Sabo and Panepinto (1990) refer to these strategies as a sex-gender system that is based on sex inequality. It represents both male domination of females and an intermale dominance. The hierarchy created may foster solidarity and conformity among males, while also assuming inequality among male groups.

CONCLUSION

When we are clear about what is operating in hazing and why, borrowing a thought from Ramazanoglu (1987) and applying it to the theme of this chapter, only then can we set about dismantling it and creating more egalitarian and humane sporting communities that are more welcoming to women and other marginalized groups. At present, most are not consciously aware of the meanings of hazing, neither those doing the hazing, nor those being hazed, nor those on the fringes such as leaders, peers, or family. This is a strength of the system. It has been built into the structure of the institution of sport in a way that deems it acceptable, normal, and innocuous. It results in a reproduction of the sport structure and culture that perpetuates abuse based upon a hierarchy seen as natural; generally, one in which males dominate other males and males dominate females.

Challenges to the practices of hazing are met with resistance. This is understandable. Attempts to transform a structure that represents hierarchy and the use of violence towards the more vulnerable initiates to maintain this structure are viewed as an assault on the traditions of sport. One university student showed he viewed such attempts as an invasion into a protected world by stating that "I could tell you the rest but I'd have to kill you" (Brian). Another, who had the courage to refuse to participate, exposed the reality of hazing by stating that "I try to avoid situations where my freedom of choice or self-respect are potentially compromised—and judging from past stories, this was going to be the case" (Annie). The critique of hazing also generates anxiety and a sense of threat as it calls into question the methods of achieving and maintaining the dominance of those currently in power. Those who have engaged in hazing practices in their past and view hazing as acceptable, or even important to team dynamics, feel threatened by the possibility of being labelled violent, and offended by the challenge to their freedoms and privilege.

In spite of many athletic departments now legislating against athletic hazing, the current trend towards the moral responsibility of athletic leaders to demand change is not taken seriously. Instead it is dismissed as a response to public concern and the need for a positive public image rather than a sincere commitment to change. This is further complicated by the fact that most athletic leaders, the majority of whom are males, are products of a system that subjected them to hazing and had them haze others. Thus, the will to change may be suspect, even when sincere. To assert their authority and assume a positive leadership position would require these individuals to acknowledge an error in past judgement. Criticism of their own past behaviours would be difficult. However, in the quest to achieve true equality and to rid the athletic institution of violence, it is a step that must be taken.

REFERENCES

Acosta, V. and Carpenter, L. (1998). *Women in intercollegiate sport: A longitudinal study: Twenty-one year update, 1977–1998.* Brooklyn, N.Y.: Brooklyn College.

Alfred University. (1999). *Report on the hazing practices of NCAA athletes.* Available at: www.alfred.edu/news/html/how_many_hazed.

Annie. (1995). *Anonymous interview: Sexual harassment in Canadian interuniversity athletics.* Unpublished manuscript.

Brian. (1995). *Anonymous interview: Sexual harassment in Canadian interuniversity athletics.* Unpublished manuscript.

Bryshun, J. and Young, K. (1999). "Sport-related hazing: An inquiry into male and female involvement," in P. White and K. Young (Eds.), *Sport and gender in Canada.* Don Mills: Oxford University Press.

Canadian Interuniversity Athletic Union. (1992). *C.I.A.U. comparative study of coaching and administrative equality.* Ottawa: C.I.A.U.

Fifth Estate. (October 29, 1997). *Crossing the line.* Canada: Canadian Broadcasting Corporation Television.

Hoffer, R. (September 31, 1999). "Praising hazing: Why it's ok to make first year players sing for their supper," *Sports illustrated.*

Holman, M. (1995). *Female and male athletes' accounts and meanings of sexual harassment in Canadian interuniversity athletics.* Unpublished dissertation. Michigan State University.

Justin. (1997). *Confidential interview: Ethics in sport and physical activity.* Unpublished notes.

Kane, M.J. and L.J. Disch. (1993). "Sexual violence and the reproduction of male power in the locker room: The 'Lisa Olson incident'," *Sociology of sport journal* 10: 331–352.

King, K. (January 31, 2003). "Doing the legwork," *Sports illustrated.*

Mandal, V. (December 11, 1997). "Hockey hazing complaints probed," *Windsor star*: 1–2.

Messner, M.A. (1992). *Power at play: Sports and the problem of masculinity.* Boston: Beacon Press.

National Collegiate Athletic Association. (April, 2002). *1999–00 Gender equity report.* Available at: www.ncaa.org/library/research/gender_equity_study.

Nuwer, H. (1999). *Wrongs of passage.* Bloomington, IN: Indiana University Press.

_____. (1990). *Broken pledges: The deadly rite of hazing.* Atlanta, GA: Longstreet.

Perry, L.A.M., Turner L.H., and Sterk, H.M. (Eds.). (1992). *Constructing and reconstructing gender: The links among communication, language, and gender.* Albany: State University of New York Press.

Ramazanoglu, C. (1987). "Sex and violence in academic life or you can keep a good woman down," in J. Hanmer and M. Maynard (Eds.), *Women, violence and social control.* Atlantic Highlands, NJ: Humanities Press International.

Robinson, L. (1998). *Crossing the line: Violence and sexual assault in Canada's national sport.* Toronto: McClelland and Stewart.

_____. (1997). *She shoots, she scores: Canadian perspectives on women in sport.* Toronto: Thompson Educational Publishing, Inc.

Sabo, D. (1987). "Sport, patriarchy and the male identity: New questions about men and sport," *Arena* 9(2): 1–30.

Sabo, D. and J. Panepinto. (1990). "Football ritual and the social reproduction of masculinity," in M.A. Messner and D.F. Sabo (Eds.), *Sport, men, and the gender order: Critical feminist perspectives.* Champaign, IL: Human Kinetics Books.

Sanday, P.R. (1990). *Fraternity gang rape: Sex, brotherhood, and privilege on campus.* New York, NY: New York University Press.

Whitson, D. (1990). "Sport in the social construction of masculinity," in M.A. Messner and D.F. Sabo (Eds.), *Sport, men and the gender order: Critical feminist perspectives.* Champaign, IL: Human Kinetics Books.

Women's Sports Foundation. (1997). *The women's sports foundation gender equity report card: A survey of athletic opportunity in American higher education.* East Meadow, NY: Women's Sports Foundation.

CHAPTER 5

Hazing, Masculinity, and Collision Sports: (Un)Becoming Heroes

Elizabeth J. Allan and Gennaro DeAngelis

Though hazing was once thought to be simply harmless pranks and silly antics, there is growing public awareness of the dangers and increasing prevalence of harmful hazing initiations among North American youth (Nuwer, 1999, 2000, 2002; StopHazing.org). In the most extensive study of hazing in college athletics (Hoover, 1999), nearly 80% of athletes reported being hazed to mark their transition to the team. Male athletes were found to be at greatest risk of the most severe and dangerous types of hazing initiations, including beatings and other types of criminal behaviour. Such hazing initiations often involve humiliating and degrading activities that can breed mistrust and a culture of abuse within a team. Sometimes such initiations result in physical injury and occasionally they are fatal (Nuwer, 1999, 2002).

In light of these problems, many coaches and educational leaders are seeking ways to eliminate hazing from their teams. Parents, teachers, and students who have seen the harm caused by hazing are also searching for answers. In this chapter, we offer an analysis of hazing among male athletes to enhance understanding of why hazing continues and what can be done to change it. Maybe if we can understand *why* athletes participate in hazing, attempts to change the behaviour will be more effective.

While hazing is not unique to the realm of athletics, hazing behaviours have been reported among sports teams at nearly all levels of play, including high school, college and professional sports teams (Nuwer, 2000). In the United States, a national survey of a sample of the over 325,000 National

Collegiate Athletic Association (NCAA) athletes (1999), found that 79% reported they had experienced some form of hazing as part of an initiation to their athletic team. In Canada, Holman (1995) and Johnson (2000, 2002) have analyzed hazing experiences of college athletes, and Robinson (1998) has described hazing experiences of hockey players in junior and professional leagues.

Hank Nuwer's work (1990, 1999, 2000) on hazing provides a platform from which to advance research on hazing within a range of contexts. Sociologist Stephen Sweet (1999) draws on the work of Nuwer and others to examine fraternity hazing from a sociological perspective. Johnson (2000) draws on the work of Donnelly and Young (1988) to analyze the subcultures of initiation practices in sport and offer alternatives to hazing. Iverson and Allan (2003) use a case study approach to provide perspectives on transforming hazing cultures in U.S. colleges and universities, and Shaw (1992) investigates hazing practices in a national study of sorority women in U.S. universities.

Descriptive statistics and narrative data on prevalence and types of hazing are important beginnings for building a body of knowledge related to hazing. However, in order to understand the complexity of any social problem, we must investigate and understand hazing in relation to its particular social context. We approach the writing of this chapter in response to this need. In order to provide more depth of understanding, we focus on the social context of athletic competition for men, and those in collision sports in particular, by applying theories of gender and athletic identity to interpret the dynamics of hazing within this realm.

HAZING AMONG ATHLETES

In sport, hazing practices are commonly referred to as "initiations," and involve a wide range of behaviours that are typically understood as rites of passage for new recruits joining a team. Hazing may involve any type of humiliating, degrading, physically harmful, illegal, or abusive behaviours, and there is much variation in the degree and scope of hazing initiations in the realm of athletics. To date, the most comprehensive study of hazing among athletes was co-sponsored by the NCAA and Alfred University in the U.S. (Hoover, 1999). While many types of behaviours might qualify as hazing, the Alfred/NCAA study used the following definition to describe initiation activities that crossed the line into hazing:

> any activity expected of someone joining a group that humiliates, degrades, abuses or endangers, regardless of the person's willingness to participate. This does not include activities such as rookies carrying the balls, team parties with community games, or going out with your teammates, unless an atmosphere of humiliation, degradation, abuse or danger arises. (Hoover, 1999)

For the purpose of analysis, the NCAA/Alfred study considered hazing within the following three categories:

- Questionable behaviours: humiliating or degrading activities, but not dangerous or potentially illegal activities.
- Alcohol-related: drinking contests, exclusive of other dangerous or potentially illegal activities.
- Unacceptable and potentially illegal behaviours: activities carrying a high probability of danger or injury, or could result in criminal charges (Hoover, 1999).

In addition to these, some of the specific hazing behaviours mentioned in the study included being yelled, cursed, or sworn at; being paddled, beaten, confined in small spaces; being kidnapped and abandoned. While many student-athletes acknowledged their exposure to these behaviours, they were often reluctant to label them as hazing per se. This may in part be due to the fact that hazing is now illegal in forty-three U.S. states (Hoover, 1999). It may also be due to students' lack of accurate information about how hazing is defined.

It is important to note that while the term "initiation" is commonly associated with hazing, the terms are not synonymous. Initiations do not by definition involve hazing practices. Anthropologists have long studied initiations and rituals as important elements of any culture. Hazing, however, carries a much more specific meaning and involves humiliating, degrading, and/or abusive behaviour expected of someone in order to become a member, or maintain one's full status as a member of a group. By its very definition, hazing excludes many positive group initiations and rituals that are not demeaning, humiliating, illegal or physically dangerous.

Of the 325,000 athletes surveyed in the NCAA study, more than 250,000 experienced some form of hazing to join a college athletic team. Of particular interest to our focus in this chapter is the finding that approximately one of every five athletes was subjected to unacceptable and potentially illegal hazing, and approximately 17%, mostly male athletes, were "deeply immersed in a culture of hazing" (Hoover, 1999). Further, "football players were most at risk for dangerous and potentially illegal hazing. They were kidnapped, beaten or tied up and abandoned. They were also forced to commit crimes—destroying property, making prank phone calls or harassing others" (Hoover, 1999: 1). The findings of the Alfred/NCAA study underscore findings described by Nuwer (2000, 2002), Johnson (2000, 2002), Robinson (1998) and others who have drawn on interviews and other qualitative data to describe hazing among high school, college and professional athletes. In these reports, as well as in anecdotal accounts and news stories, coaches are sometimes present or directly involved in the hazing initiations.

PERSONAL AND THEORETICAL PERSPECTIVES

We come to the writing of this chapter from very similar, yet in some ways very different backgrounds and experiences. We are white, middle-class, college-educated U.S. citizens working and studying at a university. We spent our childhoods and young adult years in the same region of the U.S., though a decade apart; we attended the same undergraduate institution, and we have participated in organized athletics in high school and/or college. Despite these similarities, our experiences are vastly different in many ways. These differences are due in large part to our identities as a woman and a man in a society that confers differing social expectations depending upon one's biological designation as female or male. In writing this chapter, we bring our combined experiences and expertise as a collegiate football player and coach (DeAngelis) and a decade of studying and educating about hazing, gender theory, and identity development (Allan).

While there are numerous avenues that might be pursued to advance understanding about hazing, we narrow our focus in this chapter to a scholarly analysis of athletic hazing from the perspectives of gender theory and athletic identity. While these theoretical lenses have been applied to analyze a range of issues, there have been relatively few applications of these theories to the problem of hazing. Allan (2003) and Johnson (2002) have reported on and analyzed sex/gender differences in hazing practices and have described how gender norms serve to shape and reinforce hazing traditions. In this paper, we build on these analyses to provide a more focused examination of hazing among male athletes. Our personal experiences, filtered through these theoretical lenses, have shaped our perspectives and are woven throughout this chapter.

GENDER THEORY AND ATHLETIC IDENTITY

Gender Studies is an area of scholarly inquiry that examines the social construction of masculinity and femininity and the impact of gender on individual and collective experiences in a given socio-cultural context. Research in this realm generally employs a feminist lens to examine the ways in which gender is a central organizing principle of society. A key premise of gender theory is that boys/men and girls/women are socialized to act in ways that are appropriate to their biological sex. Thus, gender theory examines how gender norms are shaped through a complex array of social forces, and in turn, how such norms contribute to shaping the social world. Since gender is understood as a social construction and learned behaviour, it is not monolithic and can change over time or across cultures or sub-cultures (Kimmel, 2000).

A number of scholars have drawn on gender theory to analyze sport as a social institution and to consider how masculinity plays a principal role in sport culture (Katz and Earp, 1999; Messner and Sabo, 1994). For example, expectations of dominant masculinity in Western societies dictate that a "real man" should be tough, strong, aggressive, courageous, and able to withstand pain. These masculine traits are reflected in the norms of organized athletics (for both women and men) and in many cases, the very definition of "athlete" is predicated upon these characteristics. Gender theory provides the lens for understanding hazing and sports initiations as gendered practices.

Athletic identity is defined as "the degree to which an individual identifies with the athlete role" (Brewer et al., 1993: 237). The concepts of identity development and performance have been acknowledged as useful in explaining role-related behaviour. The construct of identity has been recognized "as a highly relevant approach to the social psychology of sport and sport behaviour"(Brown and Hartley, 1998: 17). Researchers developed the Athletic Identity Measurement Scale (AIMS) to determine the degree to which an individual identifies with her/his role as an athlete and to measure and/or predict the relationship between athletic identity and other behaviours (Brewer et al., 1993; Hale et al., 1999). For example, scholars have examined relationships between athletic identity and athletic performance, student development in college and sport career transitions (Brewer et al., 1993; Cornelious, 1995; Hale et al., 1999).

Both positive and negative consequences of a strong athletic identity have been proposed, including the positive aspects of the acquisition of skills and the development of a salient sense of self, and the negative aspects of depression and identity foreclosure (Brewer et al., 1993; Brown and Hartley, 1998). Much of this research has emerged from the field of sport psychology and has considered the effects of athletic identity on athletes during career transitions or forced termination from their sport due to injury. Many scholars in this field contend that athletes who have a strong athletic identity are more likely to have a narrowly defined sense of self and are thus more prone to psychological trauma when their athlete role is somehow jeopardized (Brewer et al., 1993; Brown and Hartley, 1998).

When rookies are subject to hazing initiations, they are often faced with the implicit threat that they will lose their team membership or status if they do not participate in the initiation. Thus, alongside powerful peer pressure, athletic identity might also be considered a factor in the dynamics of hazing. Those strongly identified with the athlete role (with a more narrowly defined sense of self) may be more likely to participate in hazing initiations in order to achieve and maintain their status on the team. In the next section, we draw on gender theory and athletic identity as lenses for understanding one young man's experience in a collision sport. The narrative that follows is based on the experiences of co-author Gennaro DeAngelis.

MOST COURAGEOUS PLAYER

During the third quarter of the third game of my senior football season, I developed a pain in my left knee. A post-game inspection by team trainers revealed nothing to cause alarm, and I was told to ice my knee and relax it as much as possible before the start of the following week's practice. It was during that next week that the pain in my knee began to intensify, but I, not wanting to jeopardize my starting position, remained silent.

Over the next two games, as my left knee deteriorated, so too did my performance and my playing time. An X-ray and an MRI revealed nothing, and my doctors and trainers could not succinctly explain my discomfort to the coaching staff. As a result, I began to notice a change in the manner with which I was treated by some of the coaches. I sensed that they eyed me suspiciously, and a few sarcastic remarks revealed to me that they were not necessarily convinced I was even injured.

Feeling the need to prove my mettle and toughness, I continued to practice and attempted to play. I wore a cumbersome medical brace, took fistfuls of pain medication before and after practice, and even took two pain-numbing injections. Despite this, I simply could not perform effectively. My team was undefeated through seven games, and I had essentially been relegated to the role of spectator. It became apparent to me that I had become expendable, and I had become all but invisible to my coaches as well as to a large number of my teammates. I was a traitor, a weak-hearted sissy who dared admit that the pain was too much to bear. And, according to all medical authorities, there was nothing definitively wrong with me.

With seemingly nothing to lose, I opted for exploratory surgery. It wasn't until my doctor found and repaired the two large tears in my meniscus cartilage that I felt better about myself. Had I questioned my own toughness? Perhaps. However, the need to prove myself a man had not completely subsided. There were three games remaining in the season, and I was told that I would miss all of them due to my surgery. Three weeks later, with my left knee tightly wrapped and my system wrought with Advil, I played in my final game and played very well. Three months later at our team's banquet, I was given the "Most Courageous Player" award, an honor bestowed upon me by my now-supportive teammates. I felt honored, and more importantly, I felt accepted and vindicated.

Now as I sit here writing this paper at the age of twenty-six, I can feel the slightest throbbing in my left knee, a remnant of an early morning jog. I am not in constant discomfort, but I am sure that my condition will only worsen with age. When I think about what I put my body through some four years ago, I can't help but ask myself what I was trying to prove. As I am now familiar with the theory of athletic identity, it's obvious to me that I defined my existence so narrowly as an athlete, specifically a football player, that I was unprepared to have that identity stripped from me. This sudden loss caused my notion of self-worth to plummet, and any other talents or gifts that I may have had to offer paled in comparison to the importance I placed on being recognized as a successful football player.

Somewhere in my parents' home there is a plaque that reads, "Most Courageous Player, 1998." Lately I've often wondered if it should actually read "Most Foolhardy," or "Most Insecure." After all, it was my relentless desire to prove my manhood and to remain part of a group that caused me to push myself to destructive limits.

GETTING ACCLIMATED TO THE BOX

Gender theory emphasizes the role of socialization—the process by which girls and boys learn culturally appropriate norms of behaviour related specifically to their biological designation as female or male. These behavioural norms are commonly termed femininity and masculinity. Although boys and girls obviously experience the same range of emotions at one point or another, boys eventually learn that if one is to be accepted in a male-dominated society, certain emotions and actions are valued more than others. For instance, boys are more likely to be told "don't cry," and "be tough." Researchers have drawn on gender theory to analyze a wide range of experiences and societal conditions for both women and men. In this chapter, however, we draw heavily on scholars who have analyzed masculinity as a social construct.

Kivel (1999) described the rigid set of expectations associated with predominant understandings of masculinity as the "Act Like a Man" Box. The Box serves as a metaphor for the feelings of entrapment felt by many young boys as they strive for acceptance by their peers. Characteristics that are valued in order to stay in the *Box* are aggressiveness, competitiveness, anger, promiscuity, control, and responsibility. Men hoping to stay within the Box must also be financially successful, never ask for help, and above all, must never cry (Figure 5.1).

Using a box as a metaphor is also effective because of the notion of containment. Boys learn very quickly that should they attempt to step

Figure 5.1: "Act Like a Man" Box

VERBAL ABUSE:			PHYSICAL ABUSE:
	tough	have money	
	aggressive	never ask for help	
		anger	
wimp ▶	competitive	angry	◀ hit/beat up
		sadness	
girl ▶	in control	love	◀ teased
		connection	yell
sissy ▶	no feelings	intimidate	
		confusion	◀ isolated
Mama's boy ▶		low self-worth	responsible
	don't cry		
nerd ▶		resentment	◀ rejected
			take it
fag ▶	take charge	curiosity	
		excitement	don't back ◀ forced to
punk ▶		down	play sports
	don't make mistakes	isolation	
mark ▶			have sex with ◀ sexual
bitch ▶			women	assault
	succeed		

(Oakland Men's Project in Kivel, 1999: 12)

outside of the Box, they will swiftly be forced back inside with barbs such as wimp, sissy, and bitch, in addition to others. These names carry with them the inherent threat of violence, which only serves to reinforce the message that being in the Box is the safest as well as the most proper place to be.

Others have studied consequences of rigidly defined masculinity. For instance, O'Neil et al., (1986) argued that men are socialized to develop an acute fear of being associated with all things stereotyped as feminine. According to the authors, this fear of femininity is cultivated in men during their early childhood years when gender identity is being shaped and reinforced by parents and/or caregivers, peers, and media images. The fear manifests itself in men's refusal to integrate their feminine sides into their personalities.

O'Neil et al. (1986) also noted that these fears contribute to six patterns of gender-role conflict for men: (1) limited expression of emotions, (2) homophobia, (3) socialized control, power, and competition, (4) restrictive sexual and affectional behaviour, (5) obsession with achievement and success, and (6) health care problems. These behavioural patterns are meant to create distance between men and any feminine qualities they may potentially demonstrate. Independently, or in combination, these patterns would likely encourage traditionally masculine behaviours, to an extent affected by the particular context. For example, an environment that demands traditional masculinity as its desired behaviour is likely to see one or more of the six patterns of male gender-role conflict as the rule, rather than the exception. One such environment is the male athletic locker room. The locker room is considered a haven where veterans are the rulers and rookies must pledge their allegiance in addition to proving their worth. In the locker room, masculinity is held in the highest regard, and anyone straying from that standard will in many cases be put in his place by being labelled a girl or a homosexual. It is a place where stories of sexual conquest are traded and personal thresholds of pain are compared. It is partly by these processes that a social pecking order emerges among the athletes where the strongest are placed at the top and the weakest are placed at the bottom. The young man hoping to rise to prominence quickly learns the climate calls for him to exhibit a sort of *hypermasculinity* that will leave no room for questions about his athletic prowess, manhood and heterosexuality.

Collision sports, particularly football and hockey, are often viewed as avenues through which only the most masculine participants will succeed. Because the athletic definition of success is so narrow, young athletes may develop insecurities based upon the reality that only a small percentage of them will achieve traditional levels of success. This fear of failure may contribute to male athletes developing highly goal-oriented personalities where the performance of masculinity may be amplified dramatically (Messner, 1987). For example, football demands that its participants hold little regard for their own physical well-being, much less their opponents'. Messner (1987) described a young man playing football as having to "develop a personality that encourages him to view his body as a tool, a machine, or even a weapon utilized to defeat an objectified opponent" (201). This ideology can be seen in tactics employed by defensive coaches that call for defensive linemen (the first line of defense) to cause havoc at the line of scrimmage by brutally heaving their bodies into oncoming blockers. The reasoning behind such a practice is that the players behind the defensive linemen will be unencumbered towards the ball-carrier, their potential blockers now nullified by the initial collision. Such methods were often referred to as "explosions" or "train-wrecks." Coaches often speak of these maneuvers as honorable sacrifices, and some evoke images of ground troops at the invasion of Normandy or pawns upon a chessboard. Such depersonalization helps young athletes to justify actions and behaviours that would otherwise be viewed as self-destructive.

In collision sports there is an expectation that participants will continue to play despite varying amounts of pain and discomfort. Coaches often wield their players' fragile sense of masculinity as a destructive weapon in encouraging such behaviour. Miedzian (1991) suggested that the language of sport is "filled with insults suggesting that a boy who is not tough enough, who does not live up to the masculine mystique, is really a girl or homosexual" (202). In other words, if a football coach wants to encourage an injured player to compete, he may find that teasing about being a "sissy" or "fag" can serve as a strong motivator for those players whose sense of self is highly identified with societal notions of masculinity.

Relatedly, the expectation to "get it done," or succeed, by whatever means necessary, is also a staple of the competitive athlete's attitude. Players who are not willing to abide by this credo are quickly replaced by those who are. This puts the onus on the male athlete to prove to the coaches that he is more willing than the next to punish his opponent indiscriminately. By such a process, a game like football, which is already inherently violent and aggressive, becomes more so. Sabo (1994) noted that during his collegiate football career he "learned to be an animal. Coaches took notice of animals. Animals made the first team. Being an animal meant being fanatically aggressive and ruthlessly competitive. If I saw an arm in front of me, I trampled it. Whenever blood was spilled, I nodded my approval" (84). Athletes competing in collision sports are expected to take on certain characteristics in order to be effective members of the team. Our point is that male athletes, and collision sports athletes especially, are encouraged and expected to perform masculinity in its most narrowly defined sense.

Remaining inside the metaphorical "Act Like a Man" Box and having a strong athletic identity can provide many rewards in the collision sports culture, but—as previously noted—there are also many negative consequences, including injury and depression. In the next section, we describe how a hypermasculine culture, common to many collision sports teams, can provide fertile ground for degrading and often violent hazing rituals.

HAZING, MASCULINITY AND POWER

While studying the prevalence of rape by college fraternities, Martin and Hummer (1989) observed that:

> men with a broad ranges of interests and attributes are lost to fraternities through their recruitment practices. Masculinity of a narrow and stereotypical type helps create attitudes, norms, and practices that predispose fraternity men to coerce women sexually, both individually and collectively. Male athletes on campus may be similarly disposed. (470)

Such a finding speaks to ways in which highly masculine environments such as collision sport athletic teams and fraternities work to eliminate the "weaker," or less masculine, members of their groups. For both groups, hazing can be viewed as a filtering process that is used to eliminate "undesirables."

Pleck (1981) referred to this as a system of "male solidarity," through which men maintain a definition of their situation as one which not only differs from that of women, but also involves organized activities requiring the loyalty of all males. A critical point in the process occurs when men in a given group realize they have the power to exclude and discipline their members. It is with this realization that standards of social acceptance begin to take form, and the notion of the initiation rite is conceived. Within the context of an athletic team, this initiation rite often involves hazing new members as a means of marking their transition into the group.

Some proponents of hazing say such activities have made them stronger or more aware of their capabilities. For example, the following is a testimonial from a person hazed in a fraternity:

Hazing taught me to humble myself, listen to authority, interact with several people, closer than most people do with their best friend, siblings, or family. Most of all, hazing taught me my personal limits on pushing myself beyond what I ever have had to overcome. It taught me to be mentally and physically resourceful, both by myself and with others. (www.stophazing.org/pro-hazing/030999.htm)

This quotation exemplifies how traditional norms of masculinity are internalized and shape the ways in which many young boys and men come to see themselves and measure their accomplishments.

A football team is in many ways a social system with its own set of expectations. A social hierarchy exists within the group where veterans who have been members of the team the longest hold the most power, and rookies hold the least. Players who are in power have risen to that status by proving themselves the most masculine. Johnson (2001) notes that in male-dominated systems, male identification is woven into every level, and the high status positions within society are organized around qualities that are culturally associated with masculinity, such as aggression, competitiveness, emotional detachment, and control.

Sabo (1994) contends that "becoming a football player fosters conformity to male-chauvinistic values and self-abusing lifestyles. It contributes to the legitimacy of a social structure based on patriarchal power" (87). Hazing in turn can become an avenue through which this power structure can be maintained. Rookies who have been hazed are less likely to pose any threat to the power structure because they have conformed to the group by following orders and placing themselves in compromising positions for the perceived good of the group. In the eyes of the veterans, the rookies have participated in male solidarity, and have thus earned "their place" on the team.

The degree to which team members identify with the athlete role is likely to influence the nature of their involvement in hazing and the extent to which they conform to the social expectations of the team. Athletes, particularly young ones, often join an athletic team for the affiliation as much as for the physical competition. Others have built a lifetime of dreams around becoming a competitive athlete in the college or professional arena. Veterans can then exploit these desires for acceptance through degrading and often dangerous hazing rituals.

An individual who resists hazing not only runs the risk of being labelled a "weakling," but also challenges the authority of the team's power structure. For instance, if an individual refuses to be hazed, then he is disrupting a system that has served to produce that organization's system of leadership, and he is undermining the leaders themselves. Members of the team who support his stance may feel reluctant to join him because supporting him would jeopardize their own standing within the power group. This failure to speak out or to transgress against the team's power structure makes it more likely that hazing initiations will continue and perhaps intensify in the future.

It is impossible to analyze the culture of masculinity and power dynamics in sport without attending to the role of homophobia—the fear of homosexuality in oneself and others. Describing the repercussions of sympathizing with a homosexual individual or group, Martin and Hummer (1989) state, "if a member is suspected of being gay, he is ostracized and informally drummed out of the fraternity. A fraternity with a reputation as wimpy or tolerant of gays is ridiculed and shunned by other fraternities. Militant heterosexuality is frequently used by men as a strategy to keep each other in line" (461). Due to the possible backlash that may occur if an individual chooses to defy the norms of a given group, many people choose to take the path of least resistance, as it is typically the most socially acceptable path. For instance, a freshman football player, who has been strapped to a chair and instructed by his team captain to drink large amounts of alcohol, has the option to refuse. However, refusing would likely be perceived as transgressing against the team hierarchy and group norms. It is likely that such a transgression could reduce his status on the team and draw his masculinity and (hetero)sexual identity into question. According to Johnson (2001), "resistance can take many forms, ranging from mild disapproval to being fired from a job, beaten up, run out of town, imprisoned, tortured, or killed" (88). In the case of the rookie football player, he risks his status on the team. Given the importance of that acceptance, all too often this risk is viewed as more dire than any physical risk associated with ingesting massive quantities of alcohol.

Thus, it is crucial that parents, teachers, coaches and others help athletes develop the skills and provide the support necessary for making responsible choices even in the face of peer pressure. Unfortunately, students who do take a stand and report hazing do not typically find public support from peers and adult leaders (i.e., coaches, school officials, university administrators). Rather, they often find themselves ostracized from the group, subject to ridicule and/or retaliation for breaking the implicit code of silence around hazing (Nuwer, 2000). Coaches and other leaders play a crucial role in establishing norms for acceptable behaviour for team members. When hazing or other forms of abusive or disrespectful behaviour occur, coaches must take a strong stand against the behaviour and provide visible support for victims. Athletes know that when coaches "look the other way," they are implicitly condoning the behaviour. When it comes to hazing and other abuses of power within a team, coaches need to serve as role models and speak out strongly against such practices.

EDUCATION ABOUT HAZING

Related to the culture of silence around hazing, one of the major impediments to changing hazing initiations is a basic lack of understanding about the problem. Before we can expect hazing to be eliminated, we must first notice the behaviour and understand some of the problems associated with it. The following five points, adapted from a model for educating men about the problem of sexual violence (Berkowitz, 1994), can serve as a helpful starting point for thinking about a process of educating about hazing:

Help others to:
1. Notice hazing.
2. Interpret hazing as a problem.
3. Recognize their responsibility to change a hazing culture.
4. Acquire the skills needed to change a hazing culture.
5. Take action to eliminate hazing.

According to the above model, the most effective way for coaches to educate team members about hazing is to draw attention to the problem of hazing. Coaches might begin this process by providing information about the dangers of hazing and then help players develop the skills needed to take responsibility for eliminating hazing initiations. This could take a number of forms, but would likely include information about anti-hazing policies (or behavioural expectations in the absence of a formal policy); information about where to report hazing violations; assurances of support for those who do report; consequences for those who participate in hazing; and most importantly, the provision of incentives for implementing non-hazing group initiations and activities.

One of the major challenges in eliminating and preventing dangerous hazing rituals is helping team members understand how hazing initiations can hurt individuals and the team as a whole. Coaches can communicate how hazing is often predicated upon a climate of fear, mistrust and human degradation. Coaches can role-model ways to achieve team loyalty through positive non-hazing activities. The following six-point definition of hazing may be used to help athletes understand hazing as a problem:

1. Hazing is a serious problem (it is not simply harmless antics and funny pranks).
2. Hazing is about abuse of power and control over others.
3. Hazing is humiliating and degrading.
4. Hazing can result in physical and emotional harm.
5. Hazing can hurt team trust, respect, and unity.
6. Hazing is a team issue and a community issue.

Each of the above points is helpful for generating discussion and helping athletes think more critically about the potential harm that can result from hazing initiations. Point six is meant to underscore the importance of individual and collective responsibility for taking action—if hazing is an issue for the entire team and larger community (Athletic Department or school), then all members of the team and/or community have a role to play in creating positive change.

Another major challenge to preventing hazing initiations is helping team members find alternative practices to achieve the goal of inducting new players to the team. The "just say no" to hazing approach is unlikely to meet with success. Johnson's (2000) research speaks to the promising ways in which hazing cultures among athletic teams can be transformed through the implementation of team-building activities like low and high ropes courses and outdoor adventure activities supervised by trained professionals.

Ideally, designing substitute activities for hazing initiations should be a collaborative effort between coaches and players. It is possible to develop non-hazing induction rituals that will build team loyalty, respect, and trust. However, doing so will require proactive attention to the problem of hazing as well as commitment and creativity on the part of coaches and team leaders. Such a commitment will not only help to curtail the risks associated with hazing, but also likely improve positive relationships and trust among players—with the possible benefit of enhancing team performance.

(UN)BECOMING HEROES

While it is essential to promote awareness of hazing and address common misperceptions related to hazing, the dismantling of hazing in the realm of athletics requires a more sophisticated understanding of the social forces operating to reinforce hazing practices. Among these, the interconnections between dominant cultural beliefs about masculinity and the strength of an individual's athletic identity are key factors. The implementation of anti-hazing policies and educational programs is an important step, but taken alone, is unlikely to produce long-standing change.

In order to transform a hazing culture among male athletes, it is important that we consider how young boys are taught to become heroes—to perform masculinity in such a way that they earn the right to be considered "real men." Most importantly, we need to more carefully examine ways in which violent masculinity is normalized such that male aggression is often excused as "boys being boys" or "men being men." Simply put, hazing practices are reinforced by narrowly defined expectations of masculinity. If men who exemplify the "Act Like a Man" Box (Kivel, 1999) are not only rewarded, but also sometimes valorized for this behaviour, it stands to reason they would be inclined to participate in hazing—as both the hazers and hazed—because it provides an opportunity to be perceived as tough, strong, in-control, stoic and unyielding.

So while coaches and educators work to promote greater awareness of hazing and articulate strong policies and accountability measures for hazing, they can also work to recognize the ways in which cultural expectations around masculinity may undercut these efforts. Coaches can work to mitigate violent masculinity by refusing to accept (or overlook) violent and uncivil behaviour, including homophobic taunts, that tend to reinforce the "Act Like a Man" Box (Kivel, 1999). Johnson (2000) provides an extensive compendium of suggestions for "changing the initiation ceremony" to accomplish the important goals of establishing traditions and building team unity without hazing. In addition, we suggest that coaches can work to maintain competitive excellence while also understanding what it means to be a boy striving for manhood and how inherently complex this process is. For some coaches, this may be as simple as thinking back to their own experiences, and recalling their insecurity and yearning for acceptance. For others, it will require a better understanding of the cultural influences involved in how boys are socialized to be men and the possible negative ramifications of adopting narrow versions of acceptable masculinity.

In many cases, male coaches may represent a prevailing male influence in the lives of boys who are without fathers or whose relationships with their fathers have suffered during formative childhood and adolescent years. Coaches can have substantial influence on team members, and whether the influence is positive or negative may depend upon the environment a coach fosters by way of his/her actions and words.

Above all else, coaches should be wary of motivating by use of shame. Shame is a powerful catalyst upon which many coaches have struck notable results at the expense of their players' insecurities. Levant (1992) notes that in some societies, men would rather die than be subjected to the shame of violating certain sex role norms. In research that spanned centuries, Levant found that men have long viewed masculinity as an achieved state reached only through passing tests of manhood. However, the achievement of manhood is not something considered permanent. "A man can always slip back over the line. The consequences of violating these sex role norms for men are quite severe and usher in enormous shame" (Levant, 1992: 392). Thus, a coach who motivates a player by saying, "you ought to be wearing a dress" may be doing far more damage than seems apparent at the time. Even though that player might respond to such a comment by trying to prove his manhood (thereby giving the coach the desired short-term result), the coach has also planted a seed that may contribute to the player's reaction to future threats to his masculinity. More specifically, if a veteran player calls him a "bitch" when he resists a hazing initiation beating, perhaps he will be more likely to acquiesce, lest he be viewed as less than a man. Moreover, it must also be recognized that the use of such shaming is predicated upon sexism and homophobia, and thus contributes to a culture contemptuous of that which is feminine and/or gay.

CHANGING THE CULTURE

We have described the importance of effective leadership on the part of coaches and others for educating about hazing, articulating a strong stance against such practices on their teams, and supporting athletes who have the courage to report hazing rituals. We have also indicated the importance of helping athletes find ways to replace hazing initiations and traditions with non-hazing activities. In order to effectively eliminate hazing, those who work with athletes need to help generate exciting, but safe and respectful, ways for athletes to prove themselves and to build team unity without relying on the abuses of hazing.

Hazing, when unmasked, is nothing more than one group of individuals abusing power over others. Humiliation and violence are not ties that bind groups together, nor are they mechanisms by which an individual will increase his or her athletic prowess. As we have defined it, hazing is predicated upon disrespect, and thus serves to alienate people and diminish feelings of self-worth. Within the context of male sport, such effects often go unchallenged because of team members' overwhelming desire to be part of the group and to be seen as "real men."

For many athletes, hazing has become an expected rite of passage from one generation of team leaders to the next (Hoover, 1999). It can be a deep-seated tradition. However, a head coach who is an effective leader can break the cycle of hazing traditions by modelling for team members that genuine respect and unity are not fostered through abuse. Coaches and team leaders can work together to create a climate where new recruits are welcomed and where respect is earned through character development and integrity rather than dangerous hazing rituals. Creating a non-hazing team culture will likely enhance relationships among team members by building mutual respect, dignity, and trust. This possibility alone should be sufficient for coaches and team leaders to consider changing their approach to fostering unity and becoming heroes.

REFERENCES

Allan, E.J. (2003). "Hazing and gender: Analyzing the obvious," in Nuwer, H. (Ed.). *Examining hazing.* Bloomington, IN: Indiana University Press.

_____. (2002). "Hazing and athletic teams," in Kimmel, M. and Aronson, A. (Eds.). *Encyclopedia of men and masculinities*. ABC-CLIO.

Berkowitz, A.D. (Ed.). (1994). *Men and rape: Theory, research and prevention programs in higher education*. San Francisco: Jossey-Bass.

Brewer, B.W., Van Raalte, J.L., and Linder, D.E. (1993). "Athletic identity: Hercules' muscles or Achilles heel?" *International journal of sport psychology* 24: 237–254.

Brown, C. and Hartley, D.L. (1998). "Athletic identity and career maturity of male college student athletes," *International journal of sport psychology* 29: 17–26.

Cornelius, A. (1995). "The relationship between athletic identity, peer and faculty socialization, and college student development," *Journal of college student development* 36(6): 560–573.

Donnelly, P. and Young, K. (1988). "The construction and confirmation of identity in sport subcultures." *Sociology of sport journal* 5: 223–240.

Hale, B.D., James, B., and Stambulova, N. (1999). "Determining the dimensionality of athletic identity: A Herculean cross-cultural undertaking," *International journal of sport psychology* 30: 83–100.

Hoffer, R. (September 13, 1999). "Praising hazing: Why it's o.k. to make first-year players sing for their supper," *Sports illustrated*.

Holman, M. (1995). *Female and male athletes' accounts and meanings of sexual harassment in Canadian interuniversity athletics*. Unpublished dissertation. Michigan State University, East Lansing, Michigan.

Hoover, N. (1999). *Initiation rites and athletics for NCAA sports teams: A national survey*. Available at: www.alfred.edu/news/html/hazing.

Iverson, S. and Allan, E.J. (2003). "Initiating change: Transforming a hazing culture," in Nuwer, H. (Ed.). *Examining hazing*. Bloomington, IN: Indiana University Press.

Johnson, A.G. (2001). *Privilege, power, and difference*. New York: McGraw-Hill.

Johnson, J. (2002). "Are sisters doing it for themselves? An analysis of gender and the sport initiation ceremony," *Journal of Canadian woman studies/Les Cahiers de la femme* 21(3).

_____. (2001). "Taking it like a man: Re-examining the power structure in sports initiations," *Journal of culture and tradition* 23.

_____. (2000). *Sport hazing experiences in the context of anti-hazing policies—the case of two southern Ontario universities*. Unpublished Master's Thesis, University of Toronto, Toronto, Canada.

Katz, J. and Earp, J. (1999). *Tough guise*. Available at: www.mediaed.org/Media-GenderCulture/Tough Guise.

Kimmel, M.S. (2000). *The gendered society*. New York: Oxford University Press.

Kivel, P. (1999). *Boys will be men: Raising our sons for courage, caring, and community*. Gabriola Island, B.C.: New Society Publishers.

Lantz, C.D. and Schroeder, P.J. (1999). "Endorsement of masculine and feminine gender roles: Differences between participation in and identification with the athletic role." *Journal of sport behaviour* 22(4): 545–558.

Levant, R.F. (1992). "Toward the reconstruction of masculinity," *Journal of family psychology* 5(3/4): 379–402.

Martin, P.Y. and Hummer, R.A. (1989). "Fraternities and rape on campus," *Gender & society* 3(4): 457–473.

Messner, M.A. (1989). "Masculinities and athletic careers," *Gender & society* 3(1): 71–88.

_____. (1987). "The meaning of success: The athletic experience and the development of male identity," in H. Brod (Eds.), *The making of masculinities: The new men's studies*. Boston: Allen & Unwin.

Messner, M.A. and Kimmel, M. (2001). *Men's lives*. 5th ed. Boston: Allyn and Bacon.

Messner, M.A. and Sabo, D.F. (1994). *Sex, violence and power in sports*. Freedom, CA: The Crossing Press.

Miedzian, M. (1991). *Boys will be boys: Breaking the link between masculinity and violence*. New York: Doubleday.

Morin, S.F. and Garfinkle, E.M. (1978). "Male homophobia," *Journal of societal issues* 34(1): 29–47.

Nicoletti, J., Spencer-Thomas, S., and Bollinger, C. (2001). *Violence goes to college: The authoritative guide to prevention and intervention*. Springfield, IL: Charles C. Thomas.

Nuwer, H. (2002). "Athletic hazing, men's and women's sports." Available at: www.hazing.hanknuwer.com/chronology.html.

_____. (2000). *High school hazing: When rites become wrongs*. New York: Grolier Publishing.

_____. (1999). *Wrongs of passage: Fraternities, sororities, hazing and binge drinking*. Bloomington, IN: Indiana University Press.

_____. (1990). *Broken pledges: The deadly rite of hazing*. Atlanta: Longstreet Press.

O'Neil, J.M., Helms, B.J., Gable, R.K., David, L., and Wrightsman, L.S. (1986). "Gender-role conflict scale: College men's fear of femininity," *Sex roles* 14(5/6): 335–350.

Pleck, J.H. (1981). *The myth of masculinity*. Cambridge, MA: The MIT Press.

Pollack, W. (1998). *Real boys: Rescuing our sons from the myths of boyhood*. New York: Owl Books.

Robinson, L. (1998). *Crossing the line: Violence and sexual assault in Canada's national sport*. Toronto: McClelland & Stewart.

Sabo, D. (1994). "Different stakes: Men's pursuit of gender equity in sports," in

M.A. Messner and D.F. Sabo (Eds.), *Sex, violence & power in sports*. Freedom, CA: The Crossing Press.

Shaw, D. (1992). *A national study of sorority hazing incidents in selected land-grant institutions of higher learning*. Unpublished doctoral dissertation. Auburn University.

Sweet, S. (2002). "Understanding fraternity hazing: Insights from symbolic interactionist theory." *Journal of college student development* 40(4): 355–363.

Tiger, L. (1984). *Men in groups*. 2nd ed. New York: Marion Boyars Publishers.

Whitson, D. (1990). "Sport in the social construction of masculinity," in Messner, M. and Sabo, D.F. (Eds.). *Sport, men and the gender order: Critical feminist perspectives*. Champaign, IL: Human Kinetics Books.

CHAPTER 6

What's Sex Got to Do with It?

Analysing the Sex + Violence Agenda in Sport Hazing Practices

Helen Jefferson Lenskyj

The idea that male sport is the "last bastion of male supremacy" in contemporary Western society is by now axiomatic. Despite almost half a century of political organizing and activism on the part of women, sexual minorities, people of colour, and working class people, some aspects of social and sexual relations within sport remain relatively untouched by these progressive social movements.

One of the most disturbing examples of long-standing social issues in sport involves harassment and violence perpetrated by male athletes. Although the pervasive societal problem of violence against girls and women has been addressed since the 1970s in schools, colleges, universities, and workplaces, as well as in the private domestic realm, sport administrators virtually ignored the problem until the late 1980s (Brackenridge, 2001; Donnelly, 1999; Lenskyj, 1992a, 1992b). There is no shortage of examples from sport contexts, including coaches who harass or abuse girls and women; athletes who commit date rape; sport teams involved in gang rapes, particularly on university campuses; and sexual violence committed by male athletes under the guise of "hazing," which will be the focus of this chapter.

I will begin the discussion by establishing that sadistic sexual acts are a key component of many sport hazing practices, and will then develop a hazing typology based on examples from existing research. Critiques developed by Jean-Marie Brohm, Varda Burstyn, John Loy, and Brian Pronger will be examined in order to understand the sex + violence agenda in men's sport. Specifically, I will present arguments to support two key claims: first, that male sport teams function as fratriarchies, and second, that sport ideology imposes sexual discipline and repression on male athletes. Links between these functions and the homoeroticism vs. homophobia contradiction in men-only sport will be examined. Finally I will look at strategies for social change, by investigating the potential for sexual harassment policies in educational institutions and sport-related workplaces to encompass hazing. The specific sport hazing practices to be analysed here involve only male team members who are either perpetrators or victims of sexually assaultive acts that constitute part of the team's initiation rites.

It should be established at the outset that male team sports are not monolithic, and that male sport subcultures are differentiated along social class, regional, ethnic, sexual, and other lines. Equally important, progressive men within mainstream sport have been working for change since at least the 1980's (see, for example, Kaufman, 1987; Messner and Sabo, 1990), and progress has been made towards developing less violent, more inclusive, and more humane sporting forms. The problems discussed below involve worst-case scenarios in men's team sport, with (American) football producing some of the most brutal examples of hazing.

THE LEGAL SITUATION IN CANADA AND THE UNITED STATES

By mid-2002, all except seven American states had passed legislation that specifically prohibited hazing and criminalized some hazing-related offences. One example, Ohio's Bill 444, defined hazing as "doing any act or coercing another, including the victim, to do any act of initiation unto any student or other organization that causes or creates a substantial risk of causing mental or physical harm to a person." University policies typically specified outcomes such as mental or physical discomfort, embarrassment, harassment, or ridicule, and actions that demeaned, degraded, or disgraced others. Penalties included forfeiting public funds, scholarships or awards; suspension or expulsion from the university; and criminal and civil action under state law. Alcohol and recreational drugs, as well as anabolic steroid use in men's sport, were recognized in some policies for their function as disinhibiting agents that affected both the perpetrators and the victims of hazing.

Although there were parallel initiatives in Canadian universities, school districts, and sports organizations, no legislation was enacted federally or provincially. This can be explained in part by the extensive American system of athletic scholarships and the semi-professional structure of the NCAA—factors that contribute to more widespread hazing problems than in Canadian university sport contexts. There is, however, ample evidence of sport hazing in Canada as well as in the U.S. (e.g., Bryshun, 1997; Johnson, 2000).

Some anti-hazing policies stress that activities constitute hazing regardless of the willingness of the participant. In this context, peer pressure and psychological coercion are as effective as physical force—or perhaps more effective, since these methods leave no *visible* marks of abuse. In this regard, there are parallels with situations of domestic violence, where the victim stays with a violent partner for a variety of complex reasons, including the belief, often promoted by her partner in psychologically abusive ways, that she is unworthy of respect, and deserves to be treated violently because of her alleged shortcomings.

Similarly, in the subculture of men's sport, hazing mythology promotes the idea that, until they prove their "manhood" and their commitment to the team, rookies are worthy only of contempt; moreover, those who refuse to comply with hazing practices risk shame and ostracism (Johnson, 2000). While the psychological control might not be as profound or long-lasting as that exerted by an abusive partner in a marriage or intimate relationship, to the "reasonable person" outside of male sporting sub-cultures, the notion that strong and independent young men would voluntarily submit to the kinds of indignities and abuses routinely meted out by veteran athletes is difficult to understand without an analysis of the internal hierarchies of male sport.

SEXUAL VIOLENCE IN HAZING: A TYPOLOGY

The small but growing body of research studies and media reports on sport hazing practices has generated a lengthy list of examples that have been construed as hazing by the courts and/or by educational institutions in Canada and the U.S. Existing typologies tend to focus on the legality/illegality of the acts, the degree of danger or harm to victims, and the involvement of alcohol or illegal substances, as these two examples will show:

1. Initiation rites in NCAA sports teams
(four mutually exclusive categories):

    a. acceptable behaviours (only positive activities)
    b. questionable behaviours (humiliating, degrading)
    c. alcohol-related activities (drinking contests)
    d. unacceptable, potentially illegal behaviours (dangerous, criminal)
        (Hoover, 1999)

2. Initiation rites in American high schools
(four overlapping categories):

    a. humiliating hazing
    b. potentially illegal hazing
    c. substance abuse hazing
    d. dangerous hazing (Hoover and Pollard, 2000)

Rather than using these typologies, I will develop categories based on the implicit or explicit sex + violence agenda of male sport hazing practices. The examples below involve male hazing perpetrators and male hazing victims, except for those instances where male hazing victims are forced to participate in a group attack on female victims. The use of physical and/or psychological coercion to make victims comply is common to all these examples.

1. Sexual degradation

- enforced dressing as a woman, or wearing of humiliating clothing
- enforced purchase of feminine hygiene products
- enforced public nudity
- enforced shaving of testicles
- enforced full-body dyeing

Note that in a more progressive social context, taking the female role in terms of dress or behaviour might not be seen as sexual degradation, but rather as an act of playfulness, or an ironic challenge to gender boundaries. However, a key component of male initiation is distancing from and domination over women (as discussed below), and therefore enforced cross-dressing clearly constitutes sexual degradation in the context of male sport subcultures.

2. Sexual assault

- subjected to sadistic sexual assault involving one or more perpetrators (anal rape, or anal penetration with fingers or implements)
- forced to participate in gang rape (as perpetrators)
- forced to perform oral sex on veteran players
- forced to have sex with animals or multiple sex partners
- forced sexual harassment of others

3. Physical humiliation with sexual overtones

- subjected to "wedgies" (pulling up underwear)
- forced to consume non-food products, including urine or feces
- subjected to symbolic or actual subservience to veterans
- made target of sexually explicit, insulting and degrading language
- forced to self-injure or self-mutilate

In developing this typology, I have deliberately omitted the most graphic details of what are inarguably sexually sadistic practices concealed under the guise of hazing. Qualitative data illustrative of these practices may be found elsewhere in this collection, as well as in the Alfred University study (Hoover, 1999; Hoover and Pollard, 2000), Sabo and Panepinto (1990), Johnson's (2000) and Bryshun's (1997) theses, and the Stop Hazing website (www.stophazing.org).

SADISTIC SEX IN MEN'S SPORT HAZING PRACTICES

1. Male sport teams function as fratriarchies

The term "fratriarchy" describes fraternities, sports teams, and other fraternal orders or interest groups. As John Loy succinctly states, fratriarchies "bring men together, they keep men together, and they put women down." A kind of modern tribal subculture populated by young men without family responsibilities, fratriarchies promote self-interest, freedom, "the pursuit of prestige through physical prowess," and "violent, performative masculine styles" (Loy, 1995: 267). Fratriarchies exemplify hypermasculinity—the exercise of force to dominate others—as the male ideal; the concept "toxic testosterone" aptly describes the animating force in these groups (Ignatieff, 1998). As Michael Kimmel (1991: 5) explains, the relentless pursuit of a hypermasculine identity becomes a "distorted initiation process" driven by misogyny and homophobia, and exemplified by adolescent males' overinvolvement in physical and sexual assaults, gay-bashings, and gang rapes.

As the term suggests, fratriarchies have their own internal hierarchies, established in part by initiation rituals. A male university athlete in Jay Johnson's study (2000) explained that rookies needed to be taught "their place" and had to earn others' respect. Contemptuous of rookies who complained to the coach about veterans' abusive treatment of them, this athlete stated, "The rookies seemed to think that they were doing us a favor in coming to the school to play for us, and not the other way around."

While sport ideology is transmitting its own hierarchical, elitist, and authoritarian values, it diverts participants' energies away from broader issues of societal hierarchies and struggles, or, in Jean-Marie Brohm's words, the "revolt against the bourgeois order" (Brohm, 1976: 59). Instead, it poses as a system that operates on the principles of equality and merit—a level playing field, open to all, regardless of variables such as ethnicity or social class. Such myths conceal many of the crucial power hierarchies within male sporting culture, including taken-for-granted assumptions that rookies deserve to be harassed or abused as a rite of passage into the team. Thus, rookies' position at the bottom of the social hierarchy, and veterans', captains', and coaches' places at various levels above them, are both symbolically and experientially enforced through physical and/or sexual degradation.

In her discussion of the male secret societies that flourished in the early 1900s in North America, Varda Burstyn (1999: 62) explained how they were characterized by "women-distancing rituals, masculine bonding, and inter-generational socialization." By the twentieth century, sport, and militari-zation were taking over the function of conducting these kinds of male initiation rituals, the purpose of which was to eradicate maternal influence over boys and young men, and to promote hegemonic masculinity:

> Sport created an extensive, institutionalized network of social surro-
> gate and symbolic fathers and brothers-in-arms in close and ardu-
> ous physical contact—points of "libidinal cathexis" (sexual bonding)
> to use the Freudian phrase—that could provide alternative mascu-
> line points of identification against women, their sphere of domes-
> ticity, and their morality (Burstyn, 1999: 64).

Little has changed since the early 1900s; socialization into the role of male
athlete continues to demand physical toughness and emotional stoicism
(White and Young, 1999). The glorification of violence in men's professional sports—football and ice hockey, in particular—is clearly reflected
in the attitudes of owners, coaches, peers, spectators, and the mass media,
all of whom not only fail to censure violence, but often reward it.

Widespread public support for violence in sport is accompanied by
general public apathy towards high injury rates, premature retirements,
and even deaths—all part of the price that young men pay for the pur-
ported privilege of working as gladiators in the sport-as-entertainment
industry. As Greg Malszecki and Tomislava Cavar (2001: 175) aptly point
out, the prevalence and tolerance of violence in sport, and the protection
offered to its perpetrators, are "reminiscent of the discourse that used to
surround domestic abuse when it was first exposed as a tragically repugnant
way to treat significant others." Just as the private realm used to be
considered off limits to public policy and legislation ("a man's home is his
castle"), so, too, one routinely hears the call to "keep politics out of sport,"
or, more specifically, out of men's professional sport and Olympic sport
(Lenskyj, 2000). The notion that sport is apolitical—that it is somehow
protected by a "firewall" that exempts it from the level of public, political,
and moral scrutiny directed at other systems that organize social behaviour—permits some of the worst violence to continue unchecked.

2. Sports ideology imposes sexual discipline and repression

Discussing a second aspect of sport ideology, Brohm explains how sport
replaces erotic pleasure with pleasure in muscular movement, while
cultivating a "sado-masochistic type of personality, which enables the

individual to relish his own pain" (Brohm, 1976: 57).

Burstyn elaborated on this theme in her discussion of developments in Western male sport since the 1800s. Sport, like the military, became—and continues to be—a site in which "the masculine, aggressive, sexual beast" was harnessed and disciplined, so that it/he could then be celebrated. Men's physical and sexual energies were diverted away from women and the values traditionally associated with the female realm of family and relationships. Instead, boys and men were socialized in exclusively male arenas where they experienced their own masculine style of bonding, often across social class and ethnic lines.

This exclusively homosocial interaction generated a strong homoerotic dimension which continues to operate, and, more importantly, to be denied, in male sport circles. As Brian Pronger explains,

> men pit themselves against other men, using their own bodies, the bodies of their teammates and of their opponents to produce the feelings of ... embodied masculinity .... Sport offers men the opportunity to eroticize masculinity, but still maintain their orthodox [heterosexual] status. (Pronger, 1999: 190–191)

The (hetero)sexualized language of male team sports—the popularity of "penetrating-penetrated" terminology—reflects its capacity to excite those involved in sexual as well as physical ways (Burstyn, 1999: 215). At the same time, its pervasive homophobia conveniently serves to repress explicit evidence of homoeroticism—to such an extent that the public "coming out" (as gay) of male athletes, even in the more accepting climate of the 1990s and twenty-first century, still disturbs sport's orthodoxy. Ironically, it is more acceptable in most sport contexts for male athletes to "flaunt" their homophobia than to disclose their homosexuality.

As Burstyn explains, homophobia is often motivated by men's fear of "feminine" qualities —"softness, weakness, dependency, sexual receptivity" (Burstyn, 1999: 203). Football coaches, players and fans, for example, use misogynist and homophobic obscenities both to motivate the home team and to insult their opponents (Pronger, 1993). On this issue, Michael Kaufman (1987: 23) argues that men's homophobia is evident in the "obsessive denial of homosexual attraction ... expressed as violence against other men ... [which is] one of the chief means through which patriarchal society simultaneously expresses and discharges the attraction of men to other men." The sex + violence combination—that is, sado-masochism—is, in a bizarre way, a logical outcome of this process. Men's sport is ideally situated to express and discharge this attraction through legal and rule-breaking violence, on and off the field. Hazing, in particular, allows both perpetrators and victims to participate in sadomasochistic rituals that conceal the rampant homoeroticism of men's sport behind the more "acceptable" acts (in this context) of male-to-male violence.

Kaufman goes on to draw links betweeen the homophobia expressed through male-to-male violence, and the widespread societal problem of male violence against women. Similarly, Burstyn claims that the "aggressive eroticism" of men's sport—in other words, sado-masochism—also shapes heteroeroticism and heterosexual relations. Male sporting rituals and universal preoccupation with winners and losers confirm the values of dominance and submission (Burstyn), while the commodification of athletes' bodies devalues all human bodies (Brohm). In this moral vacuum, the victimization of women, gay men, and rookies is unlikely to attract sanctions.

LINKS BETWEEN HAZING AND GANG RAPE

With socialization into fratriarchies relying on group cohesion, male domination, and woman-distancing rituals, it comes as no surprise to find a significant link between fraternity or sports team membership and sexual assault. Statistics from American university campuses showed that male intercollegiate athletes were overrepresented among students who were convicted of sexual assault, including date rape and gang rape, and were six times more likely to commit crimes of a sexual rather than nonsexual nature (Bausell, 1991; Warshaw, 1988). Similar date rape patterns have been found among professional athletes (Benedict, 1998). Even members of high school teams have been implicated in gang rapes, as seen in the 1989 Glen Ridge, New Jersey case where the victim was a developmentally delayed adolescent woman. The fact that these eight young men from the school football team were seen as "heroes" made it even more difficult for the victim to be believed (Lefkowitz, 1997). (For a summary of similar examples and trends, see Lenskyj, 1992a, 1992b; Loy, 1995; Robinson, 1998.)

Research on fraternity gang rape shows how the victimization of newcomers has come to signify "the symbolic sacrifice of the self (or some part of the self) to a superior body that represents the communal identity of the [fraternity] ... the convenant promises masculinity and superior power" (Sanday cited in Loy, 1995: 271). As one of Jay Johnson's respondents explained in reference to sport teams' hazing, "Some guys like it, they get off on it ... I guess that it is the feeling of power and control you have over rookies" (Johnson, 2000).

Analyses of gang rape usually emphasize that it is a manifestation of status, hostility, control, and dominance, rather than sexual pleasure or satisfaction (Loy, 1995). However, one must ask why this display of hostility and dominance takes a sexual form, rather than simply the form of physical assault. More specifically, how is it that men's sexual victimization of other men proves their *heterosexual* superiority, and not their *homosexual* interests?

On this issue, Susan Brownmiller (1975: 197) was one of the earliest feminist scholars to examine the underlying homosexual dimensions of gang rape. The young men whom she interviewed stated that sexual excitement associated with gang rape was "largely a relationship between the boys rather than between any of the boys and the girl involved" (Brownmiller, 1975: 190). In fact, the homoerotic component is self-evident. Unlike the well-established "no prolonged staring" rules governing male nudity in locker rooms and public washrooms (Pronger, 1999: 191), a male gang rape by definition involves males watching other males engaged in sexual activity. Their attention is focused on each other, while the victim, whether female or male, is reduced to a "receptacle for institutionalized sadism," in Laura Robinson's words (1995).

HAZING = SEXUAL HARASSMENT? PROS AND CONS

Many current sexual harassment policies in Canadian and American educational settings and workplaces are based on the earlier feminist concept of a continuum of male sexual violence against women, which ranges from relatively minor forms of verbal harassment (such as inappropriate comments of a sexual nature) at one end, to violent sexual assault at the other.

By the mid-1990s, most Canadian colleges and universities, as well as many school boards, had developed harassment policies and codes of conduct, and, more recently, some national and provincial sports governing bodies followed their example. In the educational context, prevention of date and acquaintance rape among young women was a key concern in the 1980s and 1990s. Some college and university sexual harassment policies specifically included sexual assault, so that perpetrators would be subject to internal disciplinary procedures as well as possible criminal charges. Furthermore, with growing recognition of the ways in which misogyny interacts with racism, homophobia, and other forms of systemic discrimination, many policies were modified in order to address the full range of harassment. Accompanying these policy changes were educational initiatives aimed at both male and female students and employees; these included videos, print materials, posters, peer-led discussion groups, violence-prevention mentorships, and so on. At the same time, evolving policies governing alcohol use, substance abuse, orientation activities, and orientation leaders' codes of conduct helped to address the general problem of harassment. All these developments have implications for the effectiveness of strategies that include hazing under harassment policies.

An Internet search yielded numerous American school and college harassment policies that specifically identified hazing as sexual harassment, thereby including it under existing harassment policies, complaints procedures and sanctions. At present there does not appear to be any evaluation of the effectiveness of this change. It is therefore useful to review the potential benefits and pitfalls of such policy changes.

Advantages

- disrupts the "firewall" that allows male athletes to be largely exempt from harassment policies in schools and universities
- redefines the sex + violence components of hazing unequivocally as sexual harassment, subject to the full force of the law
- provides for informal as well as formal complaints and resolutions, thereby encouraging higher reporting rates
- provides definitions of sexual harassment and sexual assault, defines rights of victims, and emphasizes that "no means no"
- places responsibility on the employer, or on school/university administration, to guarantee employees and students an environment that is free of intimidation or harassment

- utilizes existing counselling and support services for victims of sexual harassment or assault
- utilizes existing anti-violence educational programs, such as the Mentors in Violence Prevention or the Athletes for Sexual Responsibility projects. (Katz, 1995)

Disadvantages

- the implicit focus of most existing sexual harassment policies is on female victims
- a male victim of sexual hazing may not define his experiences as sexual harassment or sexual assault
- the problem of hazing victims' alleged compliance remains unresolved
- the problem of hazing practices continuing "underground" is unresolved
- the nonsexual components of hazing are beyond the reach of harassment policies
- administrators, counsellors, and educators need specific understanding of male sport subculture in order to provide appropriate preventive, educational, and frontline services

CONCLUSION

It could be argued that more potential advantages than disadvantages would result from the specific inclusion of hazing in harassment policies, although it is clear that the pitfalls listed above demand attention. A multi-faceted approach to the problem is needed so that all components of hazing—from sexual violence to psychological abuse—can be effectively addressed. More importantly, there is an urgent need for broader, more radical changes in male sport subcultures. There is clear evidence that that traditional male sport ideology has dangerous consequences for women, for gay men, and for young male rookies. Interventions at all levels from local teams to national sports organizations are needed.

REFERENCES

Bausell, R., Bausell, C., and Siegel, D. (1991). *The links among alcohol, drugs and crime on American college campuses: A national followup study.* Towson, MD: Towson State University.

Benedict, J. (1998). *Athletes and acquaintance rape.* Thousand Oaks, CA: Sage.

Brackenridge, C. (2001). *Spoilsports: Understanding and preventing sexual exploitation in sport.* London: Routledge.

Brohm, J.M. (1976). *Sport—A prism of measured time.* London: Ink Links.

Brownmiller, S. (1975). *Against our will.* New York: Simon & Shuster.

Bryshun, J. (1997). *Hazing in sport: An exploratory study of veteran/rookie relations.* M.A. thesis, University of Calgary.

Burstyn, V. (1999). *The rites of men: Manhood, politics, and the culture of sport.* Toronto: University of Toronto Press.

Donnelly, P. (1999). *Who's fair game? Sport, sexual harassment, and abuse,* in White and Young, *Sport and gender in Canada:* 107–128.

Hoover, N. (1999). *Initiation rites and athletes for NCAA sports teams.* Alfred University National Survey. Available at: www.alfred.edu/news/html/rites_99.html.

Hoover, N. and Pollard, N. (2000). *Initiation rites in American high schools.* Alfred University National Survey. Available at: www.alfred.edu/news/html/hazing%5Fstudy.html.

Ignatieff, M. (1998). *The warrior's honor.* New York: Owl Books.

Johnson, J. (2000). *Sport hazing experiences in the context of anti-hazing policies: The case of two Southern Ontario universities.* M.Sc. thesis, University of Toronto.

Katz, K. (1995). "Reconstructing masculinity in the locker room: The mentors in violence prevention project," *Harvard educational review* 65(2): 163–174.

Kaufman, M. (1987). "The construction of masculinity and the triad of men's violence," in M. Kaufman (Ed.), *Beyond patriarchy.* Toronto: Oxford University Press: 1–30.

Kimmel, M. (1991). "Issues for men in the 1990s," *Changing men* 2: 4–6, 17.

Lefkowitz, B. (1997). *Our guys.* New York: Vintage.

Lensky, H. (2000). *Inside the Olympic industry: Power, politics and activism.* Albany NY: SUNY Press.

———. (1992a). "Unsafe at home base: Women's experiences of sexual harassment in university sport and physical education," *Women in sport and physical activity journal,* 1(1): 19–34.

———. (1992b). "Sexual harassment: Female athletes' experiences and coaches' responsibilities," *Sports Science Periodical on Research and Technology in Sport* 12(6), 1–6.

Loy, J. (1995). "The dark side of Agon: Fratriarchies, performative masculinities, sport involvement, and the phenomenon of gang rape," in K. Bette and A. Rutton, (Eds.), *International sociology of sport: Contemporary issues.* Stuttgart: Naglschmid, 263–282.

Malzsecki, G. and Cavar, T. (2001). "Men, masculinities, war, and sport," in N. Mandell, (Ed.), *Feminist issues: Race, class and sexuality.* Toronto: Pearson Education Canada, 166–192.

Messner, M. and Sabo, D. (1990). *Sport, men and the gender order: Critical feminist perspectives.* Champaign, Ill: Human Kinetics Books.

Pronger, B. (1999). "Fear and trembling: Homophobia in men's sport," in P. White and K. Young (Eds.), *Sport and gender in Canada.* Don Mills, ON: Oxford University Press, 183–196.

Pronger, B. (January 25, 1993). "Push 'em back," *University of Toronto bulletin* 20.

Robinson, L. (January 26, 1995). "Sick rituals purge men of all traces of femininity," *Toronto star.*

Robinson, L. (1998). *Crossing the line: Sexual harassment and abuse in Canada's national sport.* Toronto: McClelland and Stewart.

Sabo, D. and Panepinto, J. (1990). "Football ritual and the social production of masculinity," in M. Messner and D. Sabo (Eds.), *Sport, men and the gender order.* Champaign, IL: Human Kinetics.

Warshaw, R. (1988). *I never called it rape.* New York: Harper and Row.

White, P. and Young, K., (1999). "Is sport injury gendered?" in P. White and K. Young, (Eds.), *Sport and gender in Canada.* Don Mills, ON: Oxford University Press.

CHAPTER 7

Gender Differences
in Coaches' Perceptions of Hazing
in Intercollegiate Athletics

Cristina Caperchione and Margery Holman

There has been an enormous growth of literature in the area of gender issues since the 1972 enactment of Title IX, of the Education Amendment Act in the United States. This legislation mandates gender equity of resources and funding in sport and education (Lumpkin et al., 1994). However, research to date has failed to extensively examine the relationship between gender and hazing, or initiation rituals, in athletics.

This chapter is a summary of a study that examined whether or not there are differences coaches' perceptions of hazing in intercollegiate athletics based upon the sex of the coach. The study was survey research. The population was Ontario University Association (OUA) coaches. It was based upon the assumption, drawn from the histories of women's and men's sport, that female and male coaches would express differences in their views towards hazing.

The study was exploratory research. It used a survey instrument, developed from Nixon's (1994) study of coaches' perceptions of risk, pain, and injury in sport. Nixon's work, which examined the themes of "social structural constraints and inducements, cultural values, institutional rationalizations from coaches and sports management, socialization experiences and ways of accepting risk, pain, and injury in sport" (Nixon, 1994: 80), assessed whether or not there were gender differences in the way that pain is normalized in sport. The adapted version of the questionnaire, the Hazing and Initiation Ritual Index (HIRI), was developed by Caperchione and Holman for Caperchione's thesis (Caperchione, 2001) and was used in this study. It included a number of closed and open-ended statements about hazing and initiation rituals in sport to investigate gender difference in the normalization of hazing practices within the framework of the same themes.

Researchers have shown that sport predominantly operates as a male-defined and male-dominated institution (Bryson, 1987; Hall, 1993; Hargreaves, 1990) where "hegemonic masculinity is the culturally idealized form of the masculine character that emphasizes the connection between masculinity, toughness, and orientation towards competition and subservience of women" (Connell, 1987: 250). Theberge (1987) added that there is definitely an ideology in sport that is not simply about strength or superiority, but about domination, and more specifically about the domination of women by men. Traditional male sport sub-cultures tend to place a considerable amount of pressure upon participants to conform to masculinist values and beliefs. Furthermore, research has also indicated that female sport practices have become more aligned with traditionally "masculine" sports worlds (Young and White, 1995). Thus, it might follow that many females in sport would align their own traditions of hazing and initiation with those of male cohorts.

Literature (Curry and Strauss, 1994; Messner and Sabo, 1990; Nixon, 1993; Sabo, 1987; Wamsley, 1997; Young et al., 1994) has revealed that the normalization of pain is an area that parallels or represents the concept of hegemonic masculinity. Athletes who are injured, or in pain, are coerced to continue to participate because playing injured or hurt is regarded as natural or normal. It also represents the characteristics of strength, superiority and control associated with hegemonic masculinity. Pain and injuries have become normal in sports due to the individual, institutional, and social acceptance and support of athletic pain. With hazing, there is a similar acceptance of adversity and concomitant sacrifice for the promotion of team ideals. Over time, hazing ritual has become a normalized practice that resists pressure to change.

One influence that might advance a contrasting view by female coaches towards hazing is their approach to coaching and leadership. Some researchers believe that the gender of coaches may have an effect on leadership ability and style (Eagly and Johnson, 1990; Loden, 1985). Eitzen and Pratt (1989) suggested that male and female coaches differ in their philosophy and practices. They found that men expect more from their athletes in areas such as work habits, self-discipline, and attitude, demonstrating the spillover of a masculine model (Loden, 1985) that is characterized by qualities such as competitiveness, hierarchical authority, high control for the leader, and unemotional and analytical problem solving. Female sport history and the absence of hazing traditions within female sport environments led to the assumption that there would be a gender-based difference in coaches' perceptions of hazing.

FINDINGS

Coaches play a vital role in the hazing process. Based on the current study, many coaches have experienced hazing firsthand as former athletes. Others have witnessed, been aware of, or even participated in, the team hazing rituals and ceremonies of their athletes. Furthermore, coaches are viewed as leaders and role models who set standards and expectations. Thus, coaches' beliefs and attitudes towards hazing are research avenues that deserve greater attention.

SOCIAL STRUCTURAL CONSTRAINTS

Social structural constraints (SSC) refer to informal social rules, regulations or constructs that limit the opportunities of individuals or groups of people. Analysis revealed that there were no statistically significant differences between male and female coaches' responses to statements under the social structural theme of the HIRI.

The responses of the combined male and female coaches clearly sugges-ted negative perceptions of hazing under the social structural constraint theme. In a finding inconsistent with the literature, coaches failed to recognize that there are social structural constraints associated with certain aspects of sport. Generally, coaches who participated in this study did not agree that informal social rules or social norms shape the individual opportunities of young athletes with respect to hazing. Yet, coaches acknowledged that the individual need to become a part of a group or team is a critical aspect of socialization. Individuals normally feel they must conform to a certain set of beliefs developed by other group members or society in general. In sport, such socialization often involves establishing an identity as a member of a particular subculture, and having that identity confirmed by established members (Donnelly and Young, 1988). Within the subculture of sport, first-year team members or rookie athletes are forced to participate in a number of hazing activities that have been recognized as normal or traditional by veteran and past athletes. Although many rookie athletes may not agree with sport hazing, they feel obligated to participate in order to gain acceptance into the sport subculture.

In the current study, coaches claimed that hazing activities are not widely accepted or valued by athletic personnel. In particular, coaches indicated that athletes should not be expected to participate in hazing rituals when first joining a team. Veterans should, in fact, welcome first-year members on the basis of hard work and dedication. Participation in traditional rituals should not distinguish accepted members from non-accepted members. Moreover, coaches claimed that they don't turn a blind eye when hazing occurs; rather, coaches play an active role in attempting to eliminate such activities. The development of alternative socialization experiences is a strategy used to decrease rookie alienation and increase team identity (Dennis, 1998). Coaches from the current study identified alternative activities such as weekend retreats, outdoor rope courses, team meals, and weekly team outings.

Eliminating hazing practices is a goal for coaches and athletic administrators. However, reaching such a goal has been, and will continue to be, a difficult task. As much as coaches indicated their disapproval of hazing practices, athletes continue to condone it. Based on the literature previously reviewed, hazing continues to occur across North American campuses on a regular basis (Alfred University, 1999; Bryshun, 1997). Although zero-tolerance hazing policies have been created, and laws passed, athletes maintain hazing rituals by pushing the phenomenon underground. Many first-year athletes are enthralled with the traditional aspects of hazing, proposing that if hazing has continued for so many years, it must not be threatening or dangerous. Clearly, many athletes do not share the same set of beliefs towards hazing as the respondents of the current study. This may be due to the fact that athletes are unaware of the perceptions coaches have of hazing. Coaches may say they do not condone hazing practices, yet communicating this disapproval to their athletes is sometimes ineffective. As a result, the coaches' disapproval of hazing is disregarded and an athlete's choice to participate is influenced by tradition and societal norms.

Qualitative data based on open-ended comments offered by the study's participants also indicated patterns associated with social structural constraints. The following discusses the coaches' responses to questions under the social structural theme.

Question #1: Athletes should never complain

All respondents commented that athletes should complain in certain situations; some stated that athletes should always complain about athletic/team hazing. These situations included any discomfort an athlete may have with anything concerning the athletic program or concerns of health and well-being. Some who offered additional comments indicated that when athletes are in situations where they are uncomfortable, they should make it known to the coach. They also added that athletes should question first and then complain if their health and well-being are in question. When discussing sexual abuse and hazing, Dennis (1998) stated that athletes must continue to develop greater awareness of problems and discuss these problems with coaches, administrators, and other athletes.

As mentioned above, athletes have the right to inquire about anything they feel is threatening and dangerous. A study by Johnson (2000) found that student-athletes seem less interested in participating in hazing rituals due to the presence of physical dangers and humiliations of hazing. Athletes are beginning to question the relevance of such practices. In some cases, athletes are stepping forward in the fight against hazing.

A zero-tolerance policy for hazing at a number of academic institutions throughout Ontario makes it easier for athletes who want to report such incidents. Athletes are informed of the zero-tolerance policy at the beginning of each season, and know they have a venue through which to question inappropriate activities (University of Windsor, 2000).

Question #4: Unwillingness to participate in hazing results in ostracization or alienation from other team members

A majority of the respondents disagreed with the above statement. However, their response is inconsistent with the literature. Johnson (2000) indicated, "complete membership to the rank of teammate is denied until the rookie capitulates to the wishes of the team and complies with the demands of the initiation event" (87). Moreover, alienation occurs in a number of social situations where rookies or new members refuse to participate in activities designed by veteran athletes or senior members (Nuwer, 1999, 1990; Bryshun and Young, 1999; Leemon, 1972). It is not uncommon for veteran athletes to become hostile or resistant towards rookie athletes who are unwilling to participate. As a result, rookie athletes who resist are rarely granted full team membership. However, respondents suggested that those in a leadership role could control this situation. The majority of respondents indicated that the alienation of rookie teammates depends on the leadership role taken on by veteran athletes. Veteran leaders who respect the decision of a rookie to decline participation will help to eliminate alienation. Additionally, Dennis (1998) implied that coaches and veteran athletes have the responsibility to act in a manner respectful of the dignity of all participants in sport. This includes those who both do, and do not, choose to participate in hazing and initiation rituals. Based on the current study some respondents suggested that all coaches should undertake a leadership role to help deter hazing participation by first-year athletes. Despite zero-tolerance hazing policies, the final decision to participate becomes the choice of the athlete. Thus, a strong leadership role by coaches may influence the individual to decide against participation.

Question #8: Generally, coaches say they don't condone hazing rituals but turn a blind eye when they occur

Research respondents believe coaches should openly act against hazing rituals. A number of respondents commented that turning a blind eye is a cowardly act, stating that coaches are in a leadership role and need to enforce their beliefs against hazing. Furthermore, the majority of the respondents indicated that they discuss the issue every season, communicating that such practices are not condoned and never ignored.

Johnson (2000) claimed that the role of the coach concerning initiations is really divided into two categories: non-participation and participation. The coaches who are non-participants are either adamant in their demands that no initiation take place, or they feign ignorance of any knowledge of what the team is planning until after the event when they choose to acknowledge the initiation with mock disapproval or silent acceptance. The coaches who participate are either full participants or take part in a minor capacity.

Some respondents of the current study acknowledged that, unfortunately, some coaches occasionally turn a blind eye when hazing occurs. Respondent 3 indicated, "I hear of sports that do turn a blind eye, but publicly speak against hazing." As a result, coaches who decide to feign ignorance of any knowledge of the ceremonies are indirectly harming the welfare of the rookie athletes. It led to assume that the coach will turn a blind eye to the occurrence of hazing, an athlete is unlikely to feel comfortable questioning such activities. Thus, if the coach does not assume an openly negative regard for the practices of hazing, why should an athlete? In support of this, respondents strongly indicated that coaches should assume a non-participant role in the actual incident. Further, coaches must be involved in all attempts to change or eliminate such activities. As team leaders, coaches should discourage the act of hazing by devaluing its importance to the team and the athletic program as a whole. In addition, respondents suggested that coaches, in cooperation with administration, develop a series of workshops and seminars as a tool to communicate policy and educate athletes about the dangers of hazing.

Question #11: When teammates are being hazed, athletes do not consider the activities to be threatening and dangerous

Coaches studied indicated that many athletes who are being hazed do not consider the activities to be threatening and dangerous. Literature has stated that senior athletes do not consider hazing activities threatening or dangerous because they had previously gone through the same rituals and nothing had happened to them (Bryshun, 1997). As a result, these athletes support the rituals bestowed upon the new rookie members. A cycle develops where rookie athletes complete what is asked of them and prepare themselves to haze the next group of rookies (Nuwer, 1999). Each time a rookie has completed his/her hazing task and has been granted full membership, the individual quickly disregards what happened and describes the experience as a welcomed tradition. This is an unconscious way of ignoring the dangerous and degrading aspects of the experience while concentrating on the athlete's newly found group identity. Thus, athletes are oblivious to the threatening and dangerous activities that occur during hazing and initiation rituals.

Question #14: Being an athlete means you have to be willing to accept the traditions of hazing rituals

Some of the literature suggests that athletes feel they must accept hazing and initiation traditions in order to gain membership (Curry, 1989). Rookies or new group members believe that through the transformative function of ceremonies, the trials and sufferings become means for full membership into the group (Rakoff cited in Johnson, 2000). Thus, athletes feel inclined to endure or tolerate the physical and mental challenges of hazing. However, respondents do not support this premise. They strongly believe (98%) that being an athlete does not require the acceptance of hazing traditions. "Hazing has nothing to do with being an athlete" (Respondent 19). Support for this position can be found in research supporting zero-tolerance policies against hazing. "With the advent of public awareness and administrative policies, teams were no longer given the leeway to force participation of their first-year contingent in the initiation" (Johnson, 2000: 83). On the basis of visible policies against athletic hazing in most academic institutions across Canada, veterans and rookies alike are aware of the freedom to decline participation. However, even with the non-participation option available, there still exists an unspoken code that draws the participants into the ceremony (Johnson, 2000). Many individuals spoke of the pressures placed upon them by veteran members to participate in hazing practices. Others discussed the need for socialization and membership through hazing (Tiger, 1984). Moreover, a large number of athletes disclosed tradition as being a key reason for participation (Johnson, 2000; Nuwer, 1990). Thus, coaches who believe that an athlete does not have to accept the traditions of hazing may be unaware of the strength of the traditions of hazing and the pressure to conform in their athletic program.

In conclusion, coaches' responses have indicated that they are unaware of social structural constraints that support hazing in sport. Perhaps this is because coaches truly believe that hazing no longer occurs or because they feign ignorance of its occurrence. Although many coaches state their opposition to such practices, literature suggests that participation in hazing activities is a normal aspect of sport (Bryshun and Young, 1999; Nuwer, 1999).

CULTURAL VALUES

Cultural values (CV) refer to feelings, attitudes and beliefs of a certain group or organization of people. Analysis revealed that there was one significant difference between male and female coaches' responses to statements under the cultural values theme.

Like many other organizations, athletic programs promote and encourage positive cultural values such as commitment and loyalty. Coaches are recognized as leaders who serve as culture builders (Weese et al., 1993). Hazing has become a negative cultural value within athletic organizations due to its humiliating, threatening and/or dangerous nature. Yet, hazing continues to be accepted by first-year athletes, veteran athletes, and past athletes. Respondents from the current study suggested that promoting alternative socialization experiences, and incorporating safe and enjoyable activities, will build a superior team culture. In addition, respondents indicated that devaluing the traditions of hazing rituals does not diminish team cohesiveness. Moreover, coaches who oppose hazing will build a stronger team culture while helping rookie athletes feel at ease with new athletic endeavours. Weese, MacLean and Corlett (1993) claimed that "In a team sport situation, a strong and positive organizational culture will assist coaches who are interested in ensuring their 'rookies' adopt a positive work ethic and a commitment to excellence. Conversely, a negative organizational culture had the exact opposite implications for a coach" (102). Coaching and organizational (team) culture are intertwined. Coaches shape their respective team culture by promoting values that unite all team members. Devaluing hazing practices will assist coaches in developing a cultural framework employing positive beliefs and attitudes.

Qualitative data based on open-ended comments also indicated patterns associated with cultural values. The following discusses the coaches' responses to statements under the cultural values theme.

Question #6: Athletes should never question the rituals of hazing

Respondents felt that athletes have every right to question the rituals of hazing. If athletes feel threatened or uncomfortable with the activities taking place, they should question such practices. The majority of respondents

(83%) who offered additional comments stated that asking questions about such practices is a step in the right direction. Change or elimination of hazing rituals will only occur if the situation is challenged by those involved. Several commented that athletes are encouraged to come forward if any type of hazing occurs.

The next step to challenge traditions is to develop policies against hazing where none exist. If there are rules and regulations against hazing, athletes will be more inclined to question the relevance of the hazing incident, interpreting policy as organizational support. Developing a student-athlete handbook that includes the university's hazing policy is an effective way of informing athletes that hazing is unacceptable. In addition, communicating through team meetings and workshops will encourage athletes to speak out about hazing and initiation rituals. If educated about hazing and why it is not acceptable, a greater number of first-year athletes, and veterans as well, will be more inclined to share their disapproval of the practices of hazing and create alternative ways to communicate cultural values.

Question #17: Athletes who endure the physical challenges and ridicule of hazing activities deserve respect

Respondents revealed that athletes should be admired for standing firmly against hazing. "Athletes should be admired for standing up to their beliefs more than enduring hazing" (Respondent 38). Furthermore, other respondents indicated that an athlete who stands up and refuses to participate in something with which they don't feel comfortable is equally deserving of respect. However, research indicates that a small number of rookie athletes actually stand up against hazing (Bryshun and Young, 1999). Rookie athletes are fearful of what could happen to their athletic career if they choose not to participate in such activities. Johnson (2000) suggested that when rookie athletes do not wish to go through with a hazing or initiation ceremony, they are singled out and, in some cases, eventually succumb to their rite of passage. "Usually these rookies are viewed as being different or loners who do not go out of their way to socialize with the team" (Johnson, 2000: 87). As a result, membership for the neophytes is not granted as they are often ostracized and treated as outsiders (Messner and Sabo, 1990; Van Gennep, 1960), rejected for failing to be a team player.

Question #20: Generally, coaches are impressed with athletes who participate in hazing for team cohesion

Participants in the current study did not support any forms of hazing and attempted to maintain a zero-tolerance hazing policy within their athletic program. Consistent with this, the majority of respondents strongly indicated that they believe that hazing does not result in team cohesion. Respondent 3 confirmed, "I do not believe this to be true, hazing does not build team cohesion. In all actuality, hazing can disarm team cohesion." As mentioned previously, not all rookie athletes conform to hazing practices, jeopardizing full acceptance by teammates. In this event, hazing can have a negative effect on team cohesion. In contrast, recent literature has suggested that alternative activities to hazing or initiation rituals can lead to greater team cohesion. Teams that employ positive socialization experiences rather than traditional hazing ceremonies may build stronger team cultures, while forming close relationships and group identities. When the entire team participates in a controlled and enjoyable activity, team cohesion is strengthened. In the student information pamphlet from Texas A & M University (2000), coaches state that activities that promote scholarship, develop leadership, encourage community service, provide workshops on different issues, and involve campus life are all positive ways to bring teams together. In summary, coaches are impressed with athletes who are able to build team cohesion through safe and enjoyable socialization experiences rather than humiliating, threatening, and dangerous hazing practices.

INSTITUTIONAL RATIONALIZATIONS

Institutional rationalizations (IR) refer to justifications or defenses of actions by a structured agency or organization. Analysis revealed that there were no statistically significant differences between male and female coaches' responses to statements under the institutional rationalization theme of the HIRI.

The majority of combined responses of male and female participants suggested similar perceptions towards hazing statements associated with institutional rationalizations. Results under the institutional rationalization uncovered a pattern of "disagree" responses (four of six items). Many of the statements drew negative reactions to how institutions or organizations rationalize ideas, events, and circumstances. Coaches disagreed with the statement implying that athletes ought to be worried about their position on the team if they complain about hazing. From time to time coaches have to make difficult decisions concerning team selection. A number of factors come into play at the time of team selection. However, 96% of the coaches who responded to this survey were clear that participation in team hazing is not a factor they consider. Consistent with literature, respondents have certain expectations of their athletes. Some of these expectations include strong work habits, self-discipline, and a positive attitude. Commitment and dedication to the sport are also considered when joining a team (Eitzen and Pratt, 1989). Hazing does not develop self-discipline or positive attitudes; rather it creates fear and anxiety among first-year student-athletes (Bryshun, 1997; Nuwer, 1999). This may be why coaches consistently responded that compliance with hazing did not influence team selection. Athletes should, however, concentrate on developing high-quality work habits and strong positive attitudes.

Respondents from the current study also disagreed that whistle-blowers would lack public or organizational support. This concurs with Curry's (1989) point that coaches, athletic administrators and university executives totally support athletes who openly question the practices of hazing. Additionally, some media correspondents and community activists have demonstrated strong disregard for hazing rituals (*Fifth estate,* 1997). However, there are indications that hazing is supported by some individuals. Veteran athletes and past athletes believe that hazing is an important aspect of sport. They believe that it promotes team cohesion and team loyalty. Thus, athletes who blow the whistle on hazing may be praised by coaches and athletic administrators, yet ostracized and alienated by other teammates (Bryshun and Young, 1999; Curry, 1989; Nuwer, 1999). This suggests that hazing is negatively rationalized by the individuals who operate the institution or agency (coaches and administrators), and is positively rationalized by individuals central to the sport culture (athletes). Consistent with the literature reviewed, respondents suggested that coaches should encourage whistle-blowing, not as an attempt to expose individuals who are active in the hazing process, but to help eliminate humiliating, threatening, and dangerous activities, and to replace them with positive alternatives.

Qualitative data based on open-ended comments offered by the study's participants also indicated patterns associated with institutional rationalizations. The following discusses the coaches' responses to statements under the institutional rationalization theme.

Question #23: Athletes who complain about the rituals of hazing ought to be worried about losing their position on the team

Hazing should never play a part in deciding the future athletic career of an athlete. All respondents who offered additional comments clearly indicated that hazing has no part in any decisions made regarding team membership. "Hazing should never enter into this decision" (Respondent 3). Respondent 41 stated, "a coach determines who plays, if the coach is disgusted with hazing this will never be a factor." Furthermore, respondent 38 commented, "this is ridiculous, an athlete's position on a team should never be determined by this." When a coach offers a team position to a new or returning athlete, a number of factors come into play. However, participation in hazing is not one of these factors. Coaches suggested that these factors include good work habits, concentration, positive attitude, leadership, loyalty, and dedication.

In addition, respondents once again commented that coaches and administrators largely respect athletes who resist participation in hazing activities. An athlete who is able to develop a greater awareness of the values he/she believes to be meaningful is an asset to every athletic program.

Question #24: Generally, coaches and administrators do everything possible to protect athletes from hazing practices

Some respondents indicated that this is not always the case. Coaches and administrators are not able to protect athletes from hazing practices because they are unaware of the activities or turn a blind eye to them. Respondents stated that their coaches do everything possible, but generally speaking, not all coaches do. Furthermore, many coaches believe that hazing no longer exists within their athletic program so there is no need to protect athletes from hazing. "They do not do everything possible because in some programs it is not an issue" (Respondent 39). However, research has indicated that hazing does occur on a regular basis throughout intercollegiate athletics, but is masked by secrecy (Bryshun, 1997; Nuwer, 1990). In a study performed by Hunter (1995) on the prevalence of hazing in Missouri intercollegiate athletic programs, more than 50% of coaches were not aware of the hazing incidents taking place in their athletic program. Thirty-four percent of the coaches knew about the incidents but chose to ignore them. Johnson (2000) reported that the role assumed by the coach concerning hazing and initiation practices is divided into two categories: (1) coaches who are adamant in their demands that no initiation take place; and, (2) coaches who are ignorant of any knowledge of what the team is planning until after the event, when they choose to acknowledge the rituals with disapproval or silent acceptance.

Thus, coaches need to take a proactive approach to hazing even if they believe it does not occur within their athletic program. Coaches from Texas A & M University (2000) suggested all coaches educate team members and use all resources available (speakers, programs, workshops) to let members know what hazing is and why it will not be tolerated. Dennis (1998) added that coaches must take the initiative in the fight against hazing by developing, communicating, and enforcing strict policies against any forms of hazing or initiation ritual ceremonies. This will help in the elimination of hazing and in the protection of all varsity athletes.

Questions #28: Rookie athletes should trust veteran athletes

In all comments reviewed, respondents indicated that rookie athletes should trust veteran athletes under certain conditions. "Trust depends on the relationship with the veteran" (Respondent 8). Moreover, "trust must be earned" (Respondents 11 and 27). Thus, veterans must display characteristics that earn the trust of rookie athletes. For example, veteran athletes who display integrity, responsibility, and respect for other team members deserve respect. These athletes act as positive role models for new group members instilling virtues of hard work, dedication, and commitment. "If veteran athletes are good role models, they should be trusted" (Respondent 12). Veteran athletes are leaders, which differentiates them from rookie athletes. Stogdill (1974) revealed that the average individual in a leadership role (veteran athlete) is different from the average group member (rookie athlete) in the following ways: (a) intelligence; (b) alertness; (c) insight; (d) responsibility; (e) initiative; (f) persistence; (g) self-confidence;

and (h) sociability. Thus, as a leader, the veteran athlete is responsible for acting in the most distinguished manner on and off the playing ground. Veterans who support activities that are deemed humiliating, threatening, and dangerous to any group member are not acting in the best interest of the team, and thus should not be trusted by rookie athletes. To gain trust, a veteran athlete must display values, beliefs, and morals that are important to the entire team, including the rookie members.

SOCIALIZATION EXPERIENCES

Socialization experiences (SE) refer to the framing of one's perceptions by societal influences. Analysis revealed that there were no statistically significant differences between male and female coaches' responses to statements under the socialization experiences theme of the HIRI.

Socialization experiences have been defined as the framing of one's perceptions by societal influences, suggesting that the way coaches perceive things may differ due to societal influences. Based on the results of the current study, only 52% of coaches disagreed with hazing statements pertaining to socialization experiences. Coaches' disagreement suggested that hazing practices do not have to be part of the socialization experiences associated with first joining a team. More specifically, coaches indicated that one's socialization experiences might not be influenced by society. An individual's desire to participate or not to participate may be based on personal choice. Thus, athletes do not have to "tough it out" in hazing activities or go along with hazing traditions in order to gain team membership. Athletes have the choice to decline involvement when they feel participation in such activities reaches an inappropriate level. Although slightly more than half of the participants disagreed with the socialization statements, literature does not support this conclusion.

Based on the literature review, the socialization experiences of rookie athletes are influenced by society. Rarely is a rookie athlete able to choose whether or not they will be hazed (Bryshun, 1997; Bryshun and Young, 1999; Young, 1993). As discussed previously, rookie athletes are pressured to conform to hazing traditions by veteran athletes. Although many coaches strongly oppose hazing practices and do everything possible to enforce anti-hazing policies, rookies continue to participate because of the influence of others. In the current study, coaches concurred that rookie athletes will participate in hazing activities to gain acceptance. Consistent with the literature, hazing is perceived to be a traditional socialization experience within sport. It acts as a rite of passage from pre-collegiate to collegiate sport. It involves a process of indoctrination into the customary practices of a group or team by veteran athletes (Johnson, 2000). It has been a part of many cultures around the world, and is perceived as a traditional aspect of sport. As a result, rookie athletes feel obligated to play their part in the hazing ceremony. If they do not assume the role of the hazee, they may have to endure alienation throughout their athletic career.

Coaches who agreed with the socialization experience statements have implied that they are aware that hazing occurs. Although they may not support the culture of hazing, they have declared that it is present within Ontario interuniversity athletics. Furthermore, coaches who disagreed with the statements may have done so for a number of reasons. Some coaches may truly believe that hazing has been eliminated from inter-collegiate sport. Other coaches may be unfamiliar with the culture of hazing due to a lack of education about hazing or inexperience as a coach.

Qualitative data based on open-ended comments indicated patterns associated with socialization experiences. The following discusses the coaches' responses to statements under the socialization experiences theme.

Question #29: First-year athletes have something to prove

Respondents agreed that first-year athletes generally do have something to prove. They must prove they are able to play at the appropriate level and master the skills required on the playing field. "Athletes must be able to prove their skill on the practice and playing field" (Respondent 36). "On the court they do, they have to prove they can play at this level" (Respondent 19). In addition, rookie athletes must be able to work with the team and follow acceptable team guidelines.

Three of the respondents who offered additional comments indicated that first-year athletes have nothing to prove by participating in hazing. However, the coach views favourably athletes who have the courage to stand up to hazing if they feel threatened or uncomfortable. Perhaps rookies who can do this have proven to themselves and their coach that they are capable of acting responsibly under adverse conditions.

Question #34: Rookie athletes will participate in hazing activities to gain acceptance

Respondents agreed that this usually does occur. Although it may not be right, rookie athletes will participate in hazing activities to gain acceptance. "They should not have to, but where this practice occurs they misguidedly do it for this reason" (Respondent 3). Additional comments suggested that rookie athletes participate due to pressure from other teammates. All participants commented that if hazing is allowed to take place, athletes will feel pressured to do exactly as directed. Hazing and initiation rituals seem to draw participants into a situation they do not want to be in; however, these individuals will continue to participate against their own will in order to belong.

Literature has revealed that new group members feel pressured to participate due to the hierarchical structure of the group. The hierarchy is set by the veteran athletes as a means of control over the first-year players. The basis of the system is to create a tiered structure that can only be negotiated through compliance and fulfillment of ascribed responsibilities (Johnson, 2000). The hierarchy provides veteran athletes with power over rookie athletes. The only possible way for rookie athletes to find "their place" in the hierarchical structure and gain some power is to accede to the requests of the veteran athletes. The hierarchical structure has been seen as a crucial component of the hazing ceremony, not only in terms of membership or team acceptance but to convey to the neophytes their position within the structure of the team and the processes they must undergo to achieve power (Sabo and Panepinto, 1990). Thus, in order to gain complete acceptance and achieve power, rookie athletes will participate in hazing rituals.

Question #36: Athletes should expect to be hazed when first joining a team

When first joining a varsity team, athletes are overcome with feelings not only of enthusiasm and excitement, but also, in many cases, of anxiety about what lies ahead. Research suggests hazing has become a subject that elicits feelings of anxiety and discomfort amongst first-year athletes (Bryshun and Young, 1999; Nuwer, 1999). Although respondents specified that athletes should not have to worry about being hazed when first joining a team, literature has revealed different findings. In a study by Johnson (2000), interviewees stated that they all had preconceived notions that some sort of hazing or initiation ritual would take place when they first joined their varsity team. Subjects indicated they had been initiated in high school or were familiar with the practices of hazing and initiation. They also indicated that many senior high-school athletes were warned of future university hazing by past players (Johnson, 2000). Veterans expect rookies to take part in all activities leading up to and including the hazing ceremony. Accordingly, rookies expect and agree to be hazed in order to gain full membership in the team. However, respondents from the current study indicated that rookie athletes should not be anxious about hazing, rather they should be excited about being involved in different activities that help new members adapt to new environments and introduce new relationships.

CONCLUSIONS

Although specific academic literature related to hazing in sport is limited, some studies have indicated that hazing is taking place within the institution of sport (Alfred University, 1999; Johnson, 2000; Bryshun, 1997). Furthermore, these comprehensive studies have suggested that hazing practices have become a welcoming tradition for first-year athletes. However, there has been an escalation of concern among coaches and administrators regarding the pressure of hazing in intercollegiate athletics. Although research has revealed that hazing is used to consolidate the new identities of athletes and provides rookie athletes with a rite of passage to a group or team, athletic personnel have recognized such practices as abusive and threatening in nature (Johnson, 2000). Coaches and sport administrators play a vital role within the institution of sport; thus, it is necessary to further address the perceptions coaches have of hazing in intercollegiate athletics.

The purpose of this study was to investigate coaches' perceptions of hazing in intercollegiate athletics. More specifically, the researcher attempted to reveal gender differences in coaches' perceptions of hazing in intercollegiate athletics. Both quantitative and qualitative data were collected for the current study. The data were then analyzed for gender differences in coaches' responses to statements about hazing in intercollegiate athletics. Results of the analysis indicated that there were no gender differences in coaches' responses to all but one of the hazing statements. However, findings revealed patterns in combined male and female coach responses. These patterns outlined the beliefs and perceptions that coaches, in general, have about hazing within each of the four distinct themes studied. Many of the responses were inconsistent with much of the literature reviewed. Optimistically, the inconsistency may reflect changes occurring in hazing practices within Canadian university athletics through policy and education. Pessimistically, it is an indication that there is still a need for greater acknowledgement of the persistence of a traditional practice that should no longer be tolerated as we strive to generate positive cultural change within sport.

REFERENCES

Alfred University. (1999). "Report on the hazing practices of NCAA athletes." Available at: www.alfred.edu/news/html/how_many_hazed.html.

Bryshun, J. and Young, K. (1999). "Sport-related hazing: An inquiry into male and female involvement," in P. White and K. Young (Eds.), *Sport and gender in Canada*. Don Mills: Oxford University.

Bryshun, J. (1997). *Hazing in sport: An exploratory study of veteran/rookie relations*. Unpublished master's thesis, University of Calgary, Calgary, Canada.

Bryson, L. (1987). "Sport and the maintenance of hegemonic masculinity," *Women's studies international forum* 10(4): 349–360.

Caperchione, C. (2001). *Gender differences in coaches' perceptions towards hazing in intercollegiate athletics*. Unpublished thesis. University of Windsor.

Connell, R.W. (1987). *Gender and power*. Stanford, CA: Stanford University Press.

Curry, T. and Strauss, R. (1994). "A little pain never hurt anybody: A photo-essay on the normalization of sport injuries," *Sociology of sport journal* 11: 195–208.

Curry, S.J. (1989). "Hazing and the 'rush' toward reform: Responses from universities, fraternities, state legislatures, and the courts," *Journal of college and university law* 16(1): 93–116.

Dennis, P. (1998). "Harassment in sports: Implications for coaches regarding sexual abuse and ritual hazing," *CAPHERD journal* (Summer): 14–19.

Donnelly, P. and Young, K. (1988). "The construction and confirmation of identity in sport subcultures," *Sociology of sport journal* 5: 223–240.

Eagly, A.H. and Johnson, C.E. (1991). "Gender and leadership style: A meta-analysis," *Psychological bulletin* 108(2): 233–256.

Eitzen, D.S. and Pratt, S. (1989). "Gender differences in coaching philosophy: The case of female basketball teams," *Research quarterly for exercise science* 60(2): 152–158.

Fifth estate. (October 29, 1997). Canadian Broadcasting Corporation.

Hall, A. (1993). "Gender and sport in the 1990s: Feminism, culture, and politics," *Sport science review* 25(1): 48–68.

Hargreaves, J. (1990). "Gender on the sports agenda," *International review for the sociology of sport* 25(4): 287–305.

Hunter, T.G. (1995). *The prevalence of hazing within certain Missouri interscholastic athletic programs.* Unpublished master's thesis. Central Missouri State University.

Johnson, J. (2000). *Sport hazing experiences in the context of anti-hazing policies: The case of two southern Ontario universities.* Unpublished master's thesis, University of Toronto.

Leeman, T. (1972). *The rites of passage in a student culture: A study of the dynamics of traditions.* New York, NY: Teachers College Press.

Loden, M. (1985). *Feminine leadership or how to succeed in business without being one of the boys.* New York, NY: Times Books.

London free press. (October, 26, 1998). "Western pulls a sneak play on initiation antics."

Lumpkin, A., Stoll, S.K., and Bellar, J.M. (1994). *Sport ethics: Applications for fair play.* St. Louis, MI: Mosby.

Messner, M.A. and Sabo, D.F. (1990). *Sport, men, and the gender order: Critical feminist perspectives.* Champaign, IL: Human Kinetics.

Nixon, H. (1994). "Coaches' view of risk, pain, and injury in sport, with special reference to gender differences," *Sociology of sport journal* 11: 79–87.

_____. (1993). "Accepting the risks of pain and injury in sport: Mediated cultural influences on playing hurt." *Sociology of Sport* 10: 183–196.

Nuwer, H. (1999). *Wrongs of passage.* Bloomington, IN: Indiana University Press.

_____. (1990). *Broken pledges: The deadly rite of hazing.* Atlanta, GA: Longstreet.

Sabo, D. (1987). "Sport, patriarchy and the male identity: New questions about men and sport," *Arena* 9(2): 1–30.

Sabo, D. and Panepinto, J. (1990). "Football ritual and the social reproduction of masculinity," in M. Messner and D. Sabo (Eds.), *Sport, men, and the gender order: Critical feminist perspectives*, 115–126. Champaign, IL: Human Kinetics.

Stogdill, R.M. (1974). *Handbook of leadership: A survey of theory and research.* New York, NY: Free Press.

Texas A & M University. (2000). *Hazing: Some traditions are not worth upholding.* Student-Athlete Handbook/Pamphlet.

Theberge, N. (1987). "Sport and women's empowerment," *Women's studies international forum* 10(4): 387–393.

Tiger, L. (1984). *Men in groups*. New York, NY: Marion Boyers.

University of Windsor. (2000). *Student-athlete handbook*. Windsor, ON.

Van Gennep, A. (1960). *The rites of passage*. Chicago, IL: University of Chicago Press.

Wamsley, K. (July 1997). *Representations of injury and disability: The masculinizing process in professional hockey culture*. Presented at the International Society for Sociology of Sport Association conference in Oslo, Norway.

Weese, J.W., MacLean, J., and Corlett, J. (1993). "Coaches as leaders and culture builders." *Applied research in coaching and athletics annual*, 93–108.

Young, K. (1993). "Violence, risk and liability in male sports culture," *Sociology of sport journal* 10: 373–396.

Young, K. and White, P. (1995). "Sport, physical danger, and injury: The experiences of elite women athletes," *Journal of sport and social issues* 19(1): 45–61.

Young, K., White, P., and McTeer, W. (1994). "Body talk: Male athletes reflect on sport, injury, and pain," *Sociology of sport journal* 11: 175–194.

CHAPTER 8

How Sportswriters Contribute to a Hazing Culture in Athletics

Hank Nuwer

A famous poster in the 1960s declared, "If you're not part of the solution, you're part of the problem."

After conducting a computer-aided search of hazing coverage in North American sports sections from 1992 to 2002, I conclude that some sportswriters contribute to the unfortunate mindset in professional athletics which too often regards hazing as an activity that is fun, traditional, and welcome.

Such writers, and by extension the papers that publish them, do a public disservice in at least three ways.

First, since one important function of a newspaper is to introduce readers to community values, sportswriters who tolerate or promote hazing abdicate their community-watchdog responsibilities. Significantly, as hazing incidents involving high school and college athletes in the U.S.A. increasingly result in arrests, suspensions and civil suits, newspapers never fail (as far as I could find) to hold amateur athletes accountable. It is only in coverage of professional sports that some newspaper writers tolerate, or worse, encourage hazing. To be sure, some of this coverage appears outside the sports pages under local, and in a few cases, national news.

Second, since newspaper ethical codes rigidly prohibit bias in all news stories, when reporters cavalierly paint hazing incidents as harmless, they undermine the standards which professional organizations such as the Society of Professional Journalists so vigorously defend. Sports departments long have chafed under criticisms that they are little more than a newspaper's toy department, and these examples of bad hazing coverage tend to undermine a paper's attempt to deliver good, serious journalism.

Third, when newspaper editors stand idly by, allowing their colleagues free rein to promote, defend, or glamorize acts of hazing by professional athletes, these editors are at least as culpable as the school administrators who turn a blind eye to acts of hazing until an inevitable arrest, injury, or (rarely) death occurs.

In this essay, as a college journalism instructor and longtime member of the Society of Professional Journalists, I plan to point to some examples of bad hazing coverage at the professional sports level. My research and essay attempt to instruct:

1. reporters and editors to avoid such pitfalls and admonish colleagues who have lower standards;
2. readers to detect bias, error, or opinion in media coverage about hazing; and,
3. athletes and coaches to recognize the rationalizations and justifications inevitably associated with hazing.

First, let me share some relevant background information. Significantly, as I have shown in *Broken pledges: The deadly rite of hazing* (1990), newspapers have historically and, it may be argued, shamefully played a role in contributing to the culture of hazing by egging on participants in news articles and opinion pieces, as well as by emphasizing such spectacles so that whole communities could turn out to enjoy fierce "flag rushes" and "battle royals." Much of this coverage was in the late nineteenth and early twentieth centuries. Back then, only after one of these annual hazing events resulted in a death or lifelong crippling did newspaper editors condemn those whom they accused of taking a tradition too far. They quickly distanced themselves from the perpetrators and failed to apologize for the days or weeks of breathless coverage that had built up the importance of an annual initiation in the minds of spectators, school administrators, and combatants.

Long before hazing took hold in America, similar practices were rampant in medieval universities in Europe, and led to the passage of many statutes forbidding the practice. Some of these regulations can be read verbatim in Lynn Thorndike's *University records and life in the Middle Ages* (1944). Despite regulations, hazing continued in Europe long into the Industrial Age and was a persistent source of torment and injury for prep school boys at institutions such as Cambridge and Oxford.

"Fagging," a form of servitude in England that often included extortion and physical violence, was dismissed by one journalist writing for *The spectator* in 1891 (Unsigned) as "the right exercised by the older boy to make the younger do what he likes, and what the younger generally dislikes" (492). Such dismissals were especially rampant in the dozens of college and university histories (and even more conspicuous in student newspapers and yearbooks edited by undergraduates) that I have inspected since first writing about hazing in the late 1970s. Note, for example, the slanting of prose by a University of Delaware chronicler, John A. Munroe. In 1983, he condones early hazing practices, or at least defends them as "modest":

> Freshman Week grew into a useful orientation period occupying several days at both colleges. Some modest hazing was permitted, with freshmen wearing mildly ridiculous marks of their status-such as a baby rattle or teething ring on a chain; such distinctive devices served the positive function of helping members of the new class to become acquainted. [The passage may be read online at www.udel.edu/PR/munroe/chapter9.html]

Today, forms of servitude are quite common in amateur and professional athletics. For example, a non-criminal form takes place when first-year players are made to pick up veteran players' luggage at their hotels. Another current practice that dates back to medieval universities is that of new-comers, be they European scholars or rookie football players, paying for lavish meals for older scholars or team veterans. While no one is arguing that such practices as servitude or or enforcing buying of a meal are criminal (although the latter takes money out of a rookie's pocket as neatly as if his billfold were lifted), they clearly do contribute to the misguided and widespread notion that hazing is a part of tradition or the athletic culture. It also ignores the fact that experts on ritual such as Tom F. Driver (1991) have noted that often violence and ritual go hand-in-glove. This claim resonated with me in November 2002 when I read that a professional hockey player, Joe Corvo, was charged with beating and groping a female patron, a stranger to him, in a public restaurant during the Manchester Monarchs' annual "rookie initiation."

To be sure, historically, many newspapers in North America and abroad have condemned, or at least criticized, hazing practices. When a hazing death occurred or was suspected, the incident merited large, screaming headlines and, occasionally, lurid illustrations that suggested the hazers possessed demonic characteristics. This was as true in 1873, 1894, and 1899, when hazing-related deaths occurred at Cornell University, as it was in 1928, when a University of Texas Longhorn football player died from electrical shock while going through a bizarre fraternity hazing, or in 1990, when Nick Haben died of alcohol poisoning after his lacrosse club initiation at Western Illinois University. It is also important to point out that more severe types of hazing—those involving the gulping of alcohol, or improper touching of a rookie's body, or violent assault, or criminal wrongdoing (e.g., requiring new players to steal from stores or to take things from others on a scavenger hunt)—have become far more common since 1983 (though some forms of objectionable or dangerous athletic hazing certainly did occur before that date) (Nuwer, 2000: 35–36). Thus, it has taken some sports reporters and commentators such as Bryant Gumbel a bit of time to recognize (as Gumbel did in an HBO investigative piece on high school hazing in 2002) that hazing is no longer restricted to non-criminal activities such as veterans having a rookie push peanuts down a hallway with his/her nose or sing a fight song. Gumbel had formerly pooh-poohed hazing on several occasions while a morning host on the *Today show*.

My contention in this essay isn't that it is necessary, or arguably even desirable, that news reporters condemn hazing in news articles, merely that they refrain from sanctioning such practices as hazing or presenting them as acceptable, traditional diversions for veteran players.

Today, I must point out, some sportswriters in some newspapers have condemned hazing in professional sports or have quoted coaches who forbid all forms of hazing. Such news coverage is, as it should be, as objective as possible and contains quotations from those who variously condemn and defend acts of hazing. Even hazing in professional sports drew widespread critical news coverage following injuries to rookies Cam Cleeland and Jeff Danish after Cleeland was bashed in the eye with a bag of coins and Danish was thrown partially through a window and seriously cut.

The bulk of the examples I have chosen are news stories in which some sportswriters let professional coaches and athletes get away with acts of hazing. With scarcely any mention that the fight against hazing has gone on for some time in amateur hockey and high school/college sports, these writers give professional athletes/coaches the idea that what they do is somehow fun and socially acceptable, not shameful and cowardly.

There are even examples of print media endorsement hazing by teen athletes. For example, *Sports illustrated* (SI) columnist Richard Hoffer wrote an essay called "Praising hazing" (September 13, 1999) that not only implied that pro players who tape rookies to goalposts have the common sense to know when to prevent things from getting out of hand, but also made light of the so-called "atomic sit-ups" expected of some high-school rookie athletes, in which they are blindfolded and duped into doing situps so that their noses slam into a veteran's buttocks or genitals. To his credit, Hoffer warns that high school and college hazing activities ought to be verboten. On the other side of the argument, he ignores the fact that younger, amateur athletes do emulate the hazing they witness in pro sports. Because of their immaturity, there is the risk that they will take things to a dangerous extreme. It would have been only journalistically ethical for SI to run a rebuttal column mentioning the reports of high school hazing-related sodomies/sexual attacks in Massachusetts, Canada, Texas, California, Washington, and Pennsylvania, to offer a counter-viewpoint to Hoffer's smirky column in defense of juvenile behaviour.

Notably, a century ago, decades ago, and now, some of the most vigorous condemnations of hazing printed in newspapers are to be found in letters to the editor. On November 22, 1903, an anonymous letter protesting hazing "barbarity" was signed by an "American Mother" and published in the *New York times.* "By what right shall the student or company of students so maltreat one of his comrades that insanity or lifelong disfigurement or even death shall follow and suffer at most expulsion from college," she wrote. "Public spirit should rise and protest vigorously against the continuance of this practice. Let the full penalty of the law follow murder or assault or misdemeanor in the ranks of the college as it does in civic life, and hazing—often a misnomer for cruelty—will become but a hideous memory."

Compare the tone and message of the preceding letter with the implied approval of so-called mental hazing at Brown University that appeared in a front-page article, also in the *New York times*, on February 21, 1922. Note especially the word "time-honored" which clearly editorializes in a news article, as well as the apparent acceptance as fact of mere justifications for hazing offered—not by psychologists—but mere undergraduates.

Now upper class men are substituting mental torture by methods learned in psychological courses instead of by the time-honored custom of paddling. Two of the leading fraternities have adopted the new system and are pronouncing their work good. Others are expected to follow, as the results are declared to leave the initiated in a much more tractable state of mind and imbued with a "proper sense of his unworthiness."

Now let us look at some of the examples I have culled to use for instructive purposes in this essay. By no means are these examples unique; they represent hundreds of similar errors or biases that I have located in newspaper sports coverage of hazing during a ten-year period. These errors can be located in the text of some articles and in the headlines of some others. For simplicity's sake, I have broken these examples into three categories:

I. ERRORS OF OMISSION OR COMMISSION IN USE OF TERMINOLOGY

Simply stated, defenders of hazing are often eager to call their actions anything other than hazing. Journalists should not make the job easier for them by applying to hazing practices terms that fail to fit the definition of hazing. Namely, hazing involves any action explicitly required or implicitly expected of a newcomer by team veterans or coaches in which the newcomer gives up status temporarily to do something required by a veteran or veterans—willingly, seemingly willingly, or unwillingly—in order to gain acceptance and veteran status in the eyes of teammates. Such activity may be criminal (prohibited by state statute), illicit (prohibited by institution or team rules), or both.

What complicates the matter of criminal hazing is that an action prosecuted for hazing in one state or locale is not prosecuted in another because state laws on hazing vary significantly, and/or because prosecuting attorneys have shown varying degrees of willingness to prosecute such instances. Thus, occasionally, some hazing actions that probably could result in conviction and punishment go unpunished, although details of what went on may become apparent if a player or a player's family launches a civil lawsuit.

What complicates the issue even more is that some actions that involve risk and/or acts of negligence by hazers become criminal only if a victim complains, or if law enforcement officials/educators intervene when they observe such an act, or if a catastrophic injury occurs. Thus, a player asked to drink alcohol by the team may become sick, but his fellows may only face criminal punishment if the rookie is hospitalized (or, as in the case of lacrosse club player Nick Haben, dies). In fewer than half of the forty-three states with hazing laws, the willingness of the victim to participate in his own hazing is irrelevant.

All of this is irrelevant at the professional sports level, where even acts of hazing that appear to violate state law go unpunished by a team or league officials. It is especially ludicrous to me that the National Football League chooses to take no action after the two New Orleans Saints rookies were beaten by a pack of some thirty veterans, and yet the league steps in time after time to fine or suspend players for less egregious actions.

High school and college players (and casual observers) write me occasionally to ask how professional players can haze with apparent impunity, while schools expel, suspend, or in other ways punish high school or college players who perform similar acts of hazing. "Hi I'm a greek from an international fraternity, and I recently saw on ESPN Sportscenter the San Diego Chargers and Buffalo Bills hazing their rookies," wrote Joe Finn on August 23, 2002 in a letter to me. "They taped them to poles, poured ice water and Gatorade on them and made them do silly tricks. If they can do this without ANY retaliation, why can't my fraternity do the same? Because we're not rich football players? This is rude."

Clearly the question Finn poses is valid and should be asked by sports reporters and commentators, but rarely is. The ESPN coverage referred to by Finn is all the more remarkable given the network's April 2000 series on hazing in high school and college sports, which is available on its website (http://espn.go.com/otl/hazing/monday.html).

In addition, reporters and/or headline writers inaccurately refer to hazing as horseplay or pranks. More rarely, I've seen an act of negligence or prank gone wrong inaccurately called "hazing" since the prank was done by one veteran to another. On the other hand, if rookies or fraternity pledges ban together to take action against older players or members who are hazing them, that type of activity generally has been called hazing in the handful of civil lawsuits I have seen.

Here are some examples of incorrect terminology:

- A headline writer for *The Detroit news* on September 24, 2001, wrote this: "Rookies provide punch in victory over Red Sox, then endure team prank." The "prank" was hazing, albeit non-criminal, in which the clothes of rookies were removed by veterans so that the newcomers had to wear bibs and diapers upon leaving a ballpark

- In the issue of February 20, 2001, a University of Texas *Daily Texan* article headline referred to then-NBA rookie Chip Mihm's hazing as "being educated at pro level." Under no circumstances docs hazing by players a few years older than a victim constitute educating. In fact, "educating" is what the sportswriter should be doing here for the public, instead of minimizing the activity in what is purportedly a news story.

Another way in which sportswriters do their readers a disservice is by word or term choices that imply hazing is ordinary or expected at the professional level. Thus, on August 18, 2002, the *Hartford courant* referred to the "standard rookie hazing" of first-year quarterback David Carr. On December 13, 2002, The *Rocky Mountain news* refers to the practice of making rookies sing as an "old NFL hazing ritual," which is accurate but makes no attempt to inform readers that hazing is banned. Likewise, the *Florida times-union* on August 4, 2002, carried a story which asserted that "Rookie hazing is part of the lore of the NFL," the word "lore" implying that there is something time-honored or even respectable about hazing.

Then again, a sportswriter will accept a coach's assertion that hazing is banned, and then note one or two lesser indignities to which rookies have had to submit. For example, a reporter for the *Milwaukee journal sentinel* wrote on December 11, 2002, that Green Bay's Coach Sherman "won't tolerate hazing," then described the ritual in which rookies are forced to buy food and snacks for veteran players. Simply stated, reporters need to call hazing what it is and not let coaches get away with calling their teams "hazing-free" when such is not the case.

In another example, sportswriter Bob LeGere of the *Chicago daily herald* makes a point that Coach Dick Jauron considers hazing senseless. A few paragraphs later he writes:

One time-honored tradition that Jauron does permit is the rookies carrying the veterans' shoulder pads back to the locker room after practice, which he considers harmless.

This represents a critical point. Hazing endures precisely because perpetrators, whether putting their testicles on another's face, asking someone to chug grain alcohol, or merely forcing someone to endure public embarrassment, excuse their actions by saying what they've done was "no big deal" or "harmless." If a coach considers a behaviour to be harmless, he or she should then put the specific acts allowed into a team policy. Otherwise, dozens of cautionary tales demonstrate to coaches that seemingly innocent silly initiations have escalated into dangerous or illegal acts of hazing.

II. ENABLING

On occasion, sports reporters fail to offer their readers a context when they make a hazing ritual seem both ordinary and funny. A headline in the *Minneapolis star tribune* for August 14, 1998, carried a misleading message which made light of the hazing practice of tying Minnesota Vikings rookies to a goalpost. The headline made a silly play on words: "Rookies experience tape delay." Here is an excerpt from what the writer Don Banks termed "annual festivities":

> In a camp tradition nearly as old as the pigskin itself, some Vikings veterans closed their 18-day Mankato stay by taping linebacker Shawn Stuckey and cornerback Anthony Bass back to back to the goalpost after the conclusion of practice.

The story ends with a quotation that implies the reporter regards hazing as all fun and games:

> "Funniest rookie skit I've ever seen in the NFL," said quarterbacks coach Chip Myers, a 25-year league veteran.

To put this story into context, the article appeared one year after a well-publicized high school hazing incident occurred in Minnesota that resulted in the passage of a state anti-hazing law. Also in context, two days earlier, another *Minneapolis star tribune* writer referred to the players' taping of ballboys—minors—to goalposts as "fun." Kristen Davis wrote this:

> Some players have a little extra fun with the ball boys, occasionally taping them to benches and goalposts.

Davis wrote that some ballboys claim not to like the fun, and quoted one who said things are worse if they struggle. Then she quotes equipment manager Dennis Ryan, who presumes to speak for all the ballboys when, in an age of lawsuits and parental concerns about the well-being of their children, he misguidedly opines that the taping of minors to a goalpost is nothing to worry about:

> Dennis Ryan thinks they like it. "These guys have something that they can go back home and tell their buddies about, and I think they're pretty proud of that," he said.

Likewise, the *Dubuque telegraph herald* on July 31, 2001, carried this "no big deal" description of hazing when referring to the arrival in camp of then-rookie David Terrell of the Chicago Bears:

> Terrell expects a hazing period from his teammates, but says it's nothing he hasn't already endured in high school and college.

Something similar to the preceding story appeared in the *Cleveland plain dealer* on August 20, 1999. A sportswriter wrote a piece following up a claim by then-Cleveland Browns head coach Chris Palmer that hazing would not be tolerated. Instead of pointing out that the coach was hypocritical, or at least that he ran things in apparent disarray, she noted that Palmer briefly "got in on the fun" as veterans chased down and taped three first-year players to a goalpost. The sportswriter concluded her piece in a way that made it clear hazing had occurred, but included no quotations from anyone demanding that the coach ought to be held accountable. Here is how the story ended:

> Palmer explained that the rookies walked through the defensive line "and didn't respect them properly." Asked about his hazing ban, he said, "I don't know if it's technically hazing." Coulda fooled the rookies.

Unfortunately, because the "no big deal" excuse is used by hazers to justify any sort of hazing action whatsoever, reporters ought to be doubly vigilant about what they write. The following represent some of the claims made by hazers:

Asking an initiate to swim can be dangerous. A Colgate University freshman marooned on an island drowned when he tried to make it to shore. A fraternity pledge at the University of Nevada-Reno drowned in the fall of 2002 while with other pledges in an on-campus lake after midnight. A University of Texas spirit club (members fire the cannon during Longhorn football games after a touchdown) pledge named Gabe Higgins died in the Colorado River after being asked to drink alcohol and perform exercises. But here is how *The journal news,* in a well-written, balanced story, quoted Hendrick Hudson (New York State) soccer players describing the practice of marooning rookies on an island so they would have to swim for shore as "just a little joke":

> Soccer team co-captain Henry Leon said it was no big deal. "Every year, it was a tradition that we did this," said Leon, a senior. "You take a freshman, and you take them out and leave them somewhere. It was just a tradition, but we decided to change it and make it more fun ... It was no more than a 20-foot swim."
>
> "We left them in a place where they live close enough, maybe 10 minutes walking," he said. Leon said he and other players became worried when they returned in an hour, and the two students were gone. But, he added, "we knew they were definitely alive and where they were. The whole thing was totally a joke."
>
> One stranded student said 10 team members drove them to the reservoir in a four-car caravan. The teen-ager said he wasn't forced, and the entire episode "was not really that serious." "We didn't need to be initiated," he said. "The only reason we were on the team is because we were good athletes. It was just a joke, and everyone blew it out of proportion."

Likewise, in another well-written, balanced article published in *Maclean's* on March 6, 2000, a former University of Vermont hockey player says this about hazing:

> Other Canadian players maintained that this year's UVM hazing was

relatively mild compared with former initiations—but similar to what they went through in junior hockey in Canada. Benoit Lampron, now in his last year on a hockey scholarship, admitted that when he was hazed at UVM in 1996, players were stripped naked and forced to do push-ups in the freezing water of Lake Champlain—a practice that was stopped after one player suffered an asthmatic attack. As well, there was an event called "the olive run" where freshmen were made to carry olives between their buttocks while being struck with wooden cooking spoons. Lampron admits that, to outsiders, this makes the hockey players look like "perverts." But he quickly added: "This is pretty much what we do in Canada. There, it's no big deal."

Hazers have made similar claims about hazing being no big deal even after being charged with sexually assaulting a rookie. My point in using the above quotations is that sportswriters need to put claims by hazers into careful context when hazers minimize their actions or rationalize them. Perhaps the best caveat is that for years before the 1998 New Orleans Saints incident, sportswriters covering the team again and again emphasized the entertaining aspects of hazing.

For example, on August 3, 1997, Brian Allee-Walsh of the *New Orleans times-picayune* found several forms of hazing to be entertaining enough to highlight them in his article headlined "Rookies keep cool-headed during hazing"—a play on words since all rookies were given shaved heads by "razor-wielding" veterans. Here are some excerpts from Allee-Walsh's article:

- From now on, the phrase "a little off the top" will have new meaning for the New Orleans Saints' 1997 draft class. The veterans have seen to that.
- Hair today, gone tomorrow. It is the rite of passage into the NFL.
- Veterans have razzed rookies since Day 1 of the league's inception, so the goings on in Camp Ditka are typical of NFL camps. Rookies are at the low end of the totem pole. Consequently, they are required to carry veterans' helmets and shoulder pads off the practice field, fetch blocking dummies and water carts and perform other such menial tasks.

And while Coach Mike Ditka changed his tune about hazing after the injuries to the rookies in 1998 produced talk of a lawsuit, he had plenty to say about the fun and joys of hazing in the 1997 piece by Allee-Walsh: "I don't mind the razzing," said Ditka. "I think it's part of the price you pay." Ditka asked players to cool their hazing in 1998, but only because the 1997 hazing ritual had gotten out of hand and caused widespread property damage.

It isn't as if the Saints' problems as a result of hazing were anything new either. Sportswriters were well aware, or should have been, that in 1994, at a nightclub during a rookie initiation, New Orleans veteran Lorenzo Neal sucker-punched and broke the jaw of a number two draft pick, Mario Bates, after Bates refused to submit to mild servitude required by Neal, the buying of a drink.

III. ALLOWING HAZERS TO DENIGRATE THE HAZED

Reporters covering professional hazing again and again quote teammates and coaches who make fun of rookies embarrassed by the hazing they go through. Since the reciprocal nature of hazing is such that the rookies who are abused then become the abusers, these quotations in print add further humiliation to what they have already endured. And while I won't deny that a reporter has the right to use any quotation he or she obtains for a news story, I think the least a reporter can do is get quotations from experts on athletic hazing, such as Norm Pollard of Alfred University, who can put those quotations in some context. Or, perhaps even better, the reporter could quote someone such as a now-chastened former New Orleans Coach Ditka, who has come out against physical hazing in the strongest possible terms, although he did permit razzing and acts of servitude even after the Cleeland–Danish incident.

Quoting veterans who are smug or arrogant at the expense of rookies allows a reporter, in effect, to write stories that add insult to injury, or insult to insult, after a hazing has occurred. For example, here is a selection from "Giants give extreme haircuts to rookies" by Buster Olney of the *New York times* on August 22, 2002. Note the writer's use of "low-grade hazing" as if it were fact, not his opinion:

> The Giants rookie Ryan Deterding may not keep the haircut administered to him by the team's offensive linemen, and he may not fully appreciate the artistic vision required in its formation. But Deterding probably knows instinctively that no other human in the world has a

haircut like his: a shoehorn of hair cut on the left side of his head, a ragged rectangle mowed across the other side, with a tuft of hair hanging on the front, as if someone had tacked a hand broom on his forehead. Deterding was one of a half-dozen rookie linemen to get the haircuts, in a ritual of low-grade hazing. "Those guys look like the Three Stooges," Giants Coach Jim Fassel said, grinning. "That's embarrassing."

The experts in the Alfred University collegiate survey on hazing did conclude that athletes seem to be much in need of team acceptance and rituals marking player status as rookie and veteran. For that reason, Pollard and his colleague Nadine Hoover concluded that positive or humorous initiations such as skits could be acceptable, and that small symbolic acts of servitude such as carrying team balls (but not other acts of servitude such as carrying luggage) might post an acceptable boundary. Athletes themselves, and even Ditka, have argued persuasively that the singing of fight songs in camp by rookies is also a harmless tradition.

My own view is that such activities can only be acceptable if there are league and team rules that set clear limits about what is acceptable as an initiation before degrading acts of hazing take over. Such guidelines would also be useful to sportswriters, who then would have to think twice before writing news stories that put illicit or illegal acts of hazing in a favorable light.

REFERENCES

Driver, T.F. (1991). *The magic ritual: Our need for liberating rites that transform our lives and our communities.* New York: HarperSanFrancisco.

Hoover, N.C., and Pollard, N.J. (1999). *National survey: Initiation rites and athletics for NCAA sports teams.* Alfred, NY: Alfred University. Available at: www.alfred.edu/news/html/hazing_study_98.html.

Nuwer, H. (2002). *Wrongs of passage: Fraternities, sororities, hazing & binge drinking,* revised edition. Bloomington: Indiana University Press.

_____. (2000). *High school hazing: When writes become wrongs.* Danbury, CT: Franklin Watts/Scholastic.

_____. (1990). *Broken pledges: The deadly rite of hazing.* Atlanta: Longstreet Press.

Thorndyke, L. (1944). *University records and life in the Middle Ages.* New York: Columbia University Press.

CHAPTER 9

In Their Own Words:

Athletic Administrators, Coaches, and Athletes at Two Universities Discuss Hazing Policy Initiatives

Jay Johnson and Peter Donnelly

The research for this chapter was conducted at two universities and carried out in two parts. The first stage was conducted via qualitative, open-ended, in-depth interview studies with twelve university athletes. These athletes were members of various athletic teams, including ice hockey, football, soccer, basketball, volleyball, field hockey, swimming, water polo, and rugby. Data for the second part involves a content analysis of university policies on hazing in athletics, coupled with in-depth interviews with three coaches and two athletic directors. Where names have been used, they are pseudonyms to protect the identity of the individuals. As well, quotations attributed to athletic directors are denoted by (A.D.), and coaches are simply referred to as (Coach).

STUDENT-ATHLETE PERSPECTIVES ON UNIVERSITY POLICY

Students' interpretations of their respective university policies concerning the parameters of acceptable practice in athletic initiation ceremonies are quite varied. There also appears to be limited awareness of the details of the policy, although many of the athletes made assumptions about what was intended in the policy document.

> I am a little unclear as to what exactly the school policy is. I think that we are not to have initiations of any kind. They define initiations as

degradation and a lot of things that athletes don't want to take part in. (Karen)

The ambiguity of the interpretation and knowledge of the hazing policy is disconcerting, considering the fact that many of the student interviewees were, or are, team captains, most of whom were required to attend a departmental policy orientation meeting. This meeting is one of the vital links between student-athletes, administration, and coaches for the dissemination of policy information. Only 60% of the athletes interviewed admitted to knowing that their university had a policy in place, and only 20% of those participants claimed to know the contents of the policy.

Repercussions of Policy Knowledge

Despite having limited knowledge of acceptable practices, some athletes acknowledge that initiations would continue on their teams in defiance of a strict policy:

> You know quite honestly, if they are really strict on this rule, I think that a lot of the teams would ignore it still. You see everyone knows that it is still going on, even though there is a policy. (Jason)

This would seem to be a fair assessment of the present state of the approach of varsity teams towards initiations. The effect of the policy for most has meant increased discretion and secrecy surrounding the initiation to shield the administration from any knowledge of events.

> This year more than in the past, we were more receptive about not forcing people to drink, we know the acceptable limits according to the policy. We know where to take it so that no one finds out, so that no one squeals, so that word doesn't get back to the Athletic Director. We just had to be smarter about who could see. (Jenn)

Even with an admittedly weak knowledge of the specific details outlined in their university policy, the athletes still have a sense of the empathy that exists in the athletic community. They suspect that there would not be strict sanctions for their team were the administration to gain knowledge of a team hazing policy violation.

I don't know the specific repercussions of the school policy but I can see it being non-supportive and at the same time not being a very stern follow-through at all. (Winnie)

Regardless of the student-athletes' knowledge, or lack of knowledge, the initiation ceremonies continued and most participants indicated that stronger administrative directives would not change their team's customs, but simply drive them further underground.

Changes to Initiation Practices Due to the University Policy

The introduction of policies designed to curtail demeaning and harmful initiation practices, whether the Athletics Department is implementing university policy or has developed its own, has created a wide spectrum of change. On one end of the scale are examples where coaches took the initiative to completely eradicate any form of initiation or welcoming team-building activities. At the other end are teams that made no changes whatsoever in their ceremonies. The middle ground includes teams who have made some minor adjustments in their initiations in order to conform to administrative policies, while still maintaining a forum for rookie transition.

Initiation ban: For some teams, the advent of specific hazing policies has meant that they have been unable to conduct any form of initiation.

We haven't been able to initiate for two years, we haven't done anything. We couldn't have one after the "Guelph incident." It was definitely a reaction to the school policy. Basically our coach said that we couldn't single out the rookies in any type of way at all. For example, we set out to have a "Rookie Night" and our coach said no, you are not having a "Rookie Night" because of the school policy. (Sean)

From this, it is evident that it was less the university policy which influenced the team's decision than the coach's directive that nothing take place.

Modified initiations: The majority of teams researched were not specifically instructed by their coaches to cease initiation ceremonies for their rookie group. However, with the exception of two teams, all the interviewees described some former initiation practice or behaviour which had been modified to some degree. The alterations included submitting written accounts of the proposed initiation activity to the Athletic Director, moving the initiations off-campus, increasing responsibility around alcohol consumption, and the naming of the event itself.

> This year there were guys that we cut off, just because I got a little scared at the state they were in. I stayed sober, there are always two or three guys that are stone cold sober during the whole thing. I was the guy calling the shots. Before we would never cut anybody off. That is the biggest thing. Everything has stayed pretty much the same, except we don't run around the track naked. So nothing in public. No more wearing the uniform around the school. (Jonathan)

> Another initiative to counter hazing prior to the implementation of the new policy at one university was the requirement to submit an outline of the initiation activity from any teams on probation. Now we have to write what we will do for "Rookie Night" and it will have to be approved by the athletic department. That will go for every team. They want to eliminate the centering out of the rookies, and excessive drinking. The water polo team this past year had two people in the hospital for alcohol poisoning. They are looking to eliminate any kind of degrading activities. (Mary)

It should be pointed out, however, that these modifications resulted from a need to appease the Athletic Department, not to create a more welcoming inclusive environment by the team.

Movement underground: Some of changes made by teams to address the issue of the university policy on hazing are not intended to eliminate the degrading, humiliating and isolating elements of the initiation ceremony, but rather to hide their practices from public and Athletic Department view.

> We used to call our initiation, "Rookie Appreciation Night," that is, when we stopped making it other than when the whole team was there. We stopped wearing our uniforms in public and pretty much disassociated it from the school. The entire team knew that what we were doing was to make it seem that it was not associated with the school. (Yvonne)

For those teams who traditionally held on-campus activities, the policy required them to rethink their strategy to continue, while maintaining the integrity and security of the team from sanctions.

> We used to do "the run," traditionally at the University. We called it, "doing it at home," and now we just do it on road trips or at tournaments, where no one can get us into trouble away from the school where there is no risk of anyone seeing. (Jason)

The changes in initiation practices are to protect against detection, not to eliminate the practice itself.

> We instructed our rookies that no one could stay in residence because those people could tell the administration what we did. In our first year they let us into the bar dressed all goofy. The next year we could only get in dressed normally. Now we have to stay away from campus altogether to eliminate the possibility of the school finding out. That would be the end of that. (Tanja)

It would seem that alterations to policy and the strict enforcement of these changes do not go far enough towards eliminating a team's desire to perpetuate this type of activity.

No change: Only two teams noted that they had made no changes in their initiation activities due to the university's policy. One of the teams felt that their initiation ceremonies did not incur any negative sentiments or resentment from the rookie group, believing that their practices did not violate any of the new policy directives. The second team has a long-standing tradition of hazing their first-year players in a particular fashion and did not want to alter this in any way. They simply improved their methods of secrecy.

ATHLETIC DIRECTORS' VIEWS ON UNIVERSITY POLICY

Athletic directors are faced with the daunting task of not only defining acceptable initiation and orientation behaviour, but also designing policy and sanctions to curtail undesired practices. They see the coach as a multifaceted liaison between the administration and the student-athletes: the coach is responsible for the dissemination, explanation, and implementation of the policies, as well as being an agent of change for the team culture. Although many Athletic Departments are being proactive in their attempts to address this issue, there is still some resistance from within athletic administrations.

University Policies

Within the context of varsity athletics, unacceptable hazing or initiation practices are described by one Athletic Director as follows:

> Any kind of practice that would impose another's will upon a student or athlete. Where the environment that is created is one where they feel obligated through coercion to fulfill this will. They must attend and they must take part. We want to provide our students with the opportunity to team-build in a progressive, positive way that involves different skills and games, that is educational: something that will be part of a fabulous experience for the participants, not something that will establish fear or is frightening or where the athlete is left in the dark as to what they will have to endure. It should be open and inclusive. You know it should be "we are going to go to the cottage" not "we are going to get you because you are in first year." This will be the agenda. Hazing is whenever a senior or a person in a position of power, forces first-year student-athletes to go through any type of activity involving alcohol, any kind of degrading behaviour, any coercion in terms of the athlete being required to engage in an activity through peer pressure or expectation to be part of the team. What I have stated to the teams is that if you cannot in clear conscience describe what the activity was to your coach, to your family, then there is something wrong with that activity. (A.D.)

The Role of the Coach

As defined during the course of the interviews, the role of the coach is multifaceted, crucial, and at times, overwhelming. One Athletic Department, in addition to distributing the relevant policies in coaching manuals, meets with varsity coaches to outline and to reinforce the parameters of acceptable practice. It is then the responsibility of the coach to disseminate this information to her or his team. As noted by one A.D.:

> It is through the coaches that the athletes receive this information. The university policy addressing initiation practices specifically was introduced in the fall of 1996. It was made available to the coaches and it was included in the coaching manual [a handbook issued to coaches each year outlining the Department's policies]. When we first requested proposals, that was at a coaches' meeting that included team leaders, every team was in attendance. The student leaders also received a copy of the policy. I think that down the road we could ameliorate the dissemination of this information. That is what we have done up to this point to try and get it to the student leaders. (A.D.)

There is, however, an expectation from the administration that coaches will assume an increasingly proactive role in changing the existing structure of varsity initiation practices.

> The coaches have to take a very active role. They have to make it very clear, not only what the policy is but also what the intentions are. What is behind the policy, why is it that we are taking this kind of position. Then engage in dialogue with the athletes to find solutions. To find other ways of looking at team building. The problem is that some of these guys, (I say guys but it is both and that is very clear in the literature), they refer to it as team building, they refer to it as a bonding experience, but ultimately they do see it as a rite of passage. It is the rite of passage that we want to eliminate. Get into really productive team building activities. If we can get there we will have overcome years and years of not just stereotypes but a lot of past practice. (A.D.)

While the coach is viewed as the primary vehicle for change, the administration acknowledges that it is asking a frustrating, nearly insurmountable task of the coach:

> The coaches are also very frustrated. They have been a part of the

attempt to change it [hazing] over a long period of time. They have been the ones who are coming forward and saying unless there are sanctions then it is only talk and they are not going to get the change. More coaches, in terms of the sanctions that we imposed this year, are at least saying that they know that we are serious. The coaches are going through the same workshops that the athletes go through. Early on we had mass workshops, all the coaches saw an educational video ("Chuck"), all the coaches have gone through the codes of conduct, both the student code of conduct and the athletic code of conduct. What I am finding is that the coaches all know what the issues are but what we haven't been able to effectively provide them with is an implementation for change. That is where we are at now and struggling with looking at a change agent. That is where we feel we need to bring in an expert from outside who has expertise in that area. (A.D.)

It is clear that the Athletic Directors understand that coaches need directives and guides to successfully negotiate change within the present system, and the coaches feel that they are in need of stronger sanctions to drive home the message of zero tolerance to the athletes.

The role of the coach is double: he or she is seen both as an agent of change, and as someone who supports and encourages the continuation of traditional initiations. This position severely limits and weakens the authority of the Athletic Department to usher in a new era of student-athlete orientation—one which is inclusive, rather than exclusive and segregational.

We may still have people involved who think that it is an important part of the varsity experience. It is a huge part of the problem. If you don't do it (go through with the initiation). I can tell you that there are students who will not participate, who will not attend institutions and are not participating in sport because of it, and I think that is an awful shame. Likewise there are also students participating that don't want to be, but feel obligated. (A.D.)

The Athletic Directors acknowledge that, within their own ranks, there are still coaches who believe that the initiation ceremony is worth preserving, and should continue to be an integral component of their team.

The Sport Culture

One of the Athletic Directors interviewed described other Athletic Directors and their positions concerning initiation practices as fitting into three distinct groups.

1. There are some administrators who know that this is going on and they have had incidents, and they choose not to dig because scratching the surface will only cause more problems for themselves. The directors that are in our league and in positions of authority—there are probably very few like that.
2. Most probably know that something is going on but are very frustrated because they don't know how to get to it.
3. The third group honestly just doesn't know. (A.D.)

These varied views from athletic departments, either unwilling to explore, unable to intervene, or oblivious to any existing problems, constantly undermine concerned groups attempting to address the issues surrounding initiations. There is a shroud of secrecy surrounding these traditions, creating an environment in which information is not shared with outsiders who are perceived to be attempting to unravel a system which seeks only to protect its membership.

There is also an oppositional relationship between the sport culture and the greater community, one which came to light with media reports of initiation and hazing stories at two universities in Ontario. Two different approaches were adopted by university administrations. One chose to be forthcoming and pre-empted media speculation and gossip by releasing the details of the initiation events. The second chose not to release any information about the incident, leading to both public and media condemnation.

The feedback that we have gotten back from the media has been interesting. There is quite a difference between how the incident here and the incident at Western University have been addressed in the media. The phone calls, the editorials that were there, people really wanted to see a change. It is not isolated programs. The programs where it is evident are the programs where there is a proactive actual investigation of incidents. In some cases it is simply a report that this occurred, it is investigated and more information is brought forward. That is exactly what happened at Western University. It was a call to the hazing hotline [like ours]. When that is reported we do a thorough investigation. (A.D.)

It was evident through the differing approaches that the code of secrecy extends beyond the team. For some, the community encompasses coaches, players and administrators, and resistance to change often comes from those who have gone through, or have been a part of, initiation processes themselves. This was an initiative by a football team as an alternative to hazing:

Our football team went away to a training camp. It was interesting talking to some of the alumni, they would say things like, why would we spend all of that money on that [alternative orientation events such as ropes courses]. It was in fact raised by students and fundraising. The kids all wanted to do this. Talking to the football players today, that was the highlight of their year. It was interesting hearing the alumni saying that. When they reminisce this is what they remember. Their perception was that the initiation was an integral part of their years as football players. (A.D.)

In order for fundamental change to take place in initiation practices, all members of the community, players, administrators, coaches, and perhaps even alumni/ae must be on board with the philosophy. They need to understand the importance of support from all.

Administrative Procedural Steps

The two university and athletic administrations in this study have four main methods for dealing with initiation and hazing complaints: reporting, education, sanctions (probation, forfeitures), and alternative choices. They are also undertaking a joint effort with the Offices of the Athletic Directors and Student Affairs to combat hazing.

Reporting: The first line of intervention regarding initiation violations is reporting. This is accomplished through educational seminars designed to educate and create awareness for the support staff of the university. Some universities have established hazing hotlines: phones that provide a direct link between the university community and the university administration.

The intention of such communications is to facilitate the transmission of sensitive information. The caller can remain anonymous and still precipitate an investigation into alleged infractions.

Education: With the onset of public scrutiny into initiation and hazing practices in the military, fraternity and sorority organizations, and varsity and sporting cultures, universities have been obliged to address this issue at a policy level. A second step has been the creation of seminars designed to educate players, coaches, and team leaders to the dangers of initiations. This can also involve the viewing of educational videos such as "Chuck" (the story of a mother whose son died in a hazing-related incident, and who is determined to inform the public of the hazards of initiations) and "Hazed and confused: Changing the hazing culture in varsity athletics" (a documentary that highlights both the negative outcomes of some current sport hazing practices as well as the progressive successes of alternative orientation ceremonies such as camping excursions and ropes courses) (Johnson, 2000).

Sanctions: Few universities have found themselves in the position of having to enforce any sort of disciplinary action for sport hazing infractions. However, over the course of the last five years, Guelph University, the University of Western Ontario, the University of British Columbia, Brock University, the University of Vermont, the University of New Brunswick, and McMaster University have been the focus of initiation incidents that became public knowledge. In the case of Guelph, the head coach of men's hockey was suspended for one game for allowing alcohol in the dressing room. At Western, the head football coach suspended himself for the remaining 1998 league games (a period of two pre-playoff games), feeling that that was an adequate penalty for the actions of his team. McMaster, which has had several teams on probation, suspended two of their varsity teams in 1999 for one league game each. Community service was also imposed on the two penalized McMaster teams. This involved the design and implementation of educational programs about hazing at the feeder-school level. The teams were also required to undergo two educational seminars concerning the issues of hazing in athletics.

With the ongoing motivation of teams to initiate their first-year contingent, strong sanctions are seen by some as a necessary deterrence, as evidenced in the actions taken by McMaster University. This approach, however, which saw the forfeiture of two league games, is viewed as having ramifications for the other teams in the league, affecting the integrity of the divisions to which they belonged.

The sanction of forfeiting a match is a decision that I really question. It really affects the integrity of the entire league. These are sanctions which were imposed on two teams at a University this season. Losing a game is easy, but to me it is much bigger than that. It affects the league. I don't necessarily feel that the actions of the student-athletes at one university should affect all of the athletes in Ontario. I think that their actions should affect themselves and in turn should also affect all of our programs to make sure that our student-athletes and coaches are aware. We have to be concerned about what is happening in our own house and how we are handling that. If we have a team that is not following policy then we have to get them (a) following the policy and (b) understanding what the consequences will be if they are not following the policy. (A.D.)

The two A.D.s interviewed are attempting to deal with initiation infractions from within:

The one thing that you want to do with sanctions is that you want them to happen from within. You want the team building to take place. You could put together a program (for that team) on team building. That could be part of it, whether that be a public service, there are so many things to do. We could put together something for them where they are doing a public service within the university, where they are working together as a team. As far as probation or suspensions that could also be a part of it depending on the severity of the case, but I would think that first and foremost in my mind we would ensure that part of the solution would include appropriate team building and that we would support it. That would be number one. Number two, you could be looking at probationary suspensions of members of the team, of coaches, the entire team, really the full gamut. This is all dependent on the severity of the infraction of the case that we are presented with. (A.D.)

Even with various progressive administrative attempts to curtail initiations, the A.D.s concede that the problem will continue to exist, in part due to a deeply entrenched belief system:

> I think that it is going to take a great deal more time to change the belief system of our current athletes who have really had a lifetime within sports of this kind of activity, this part of being a member of a team. To expect that we will be able to change that belief system and that they will then be able to go into the schools in this current year and make an impact is somewhat naïve. So we are focusing more on a workshop where we invite speakers, varsity athletes, and representatives from the high schools to come. I would also like to work with universities which are actively searching for solutions. (A.D.)

It is difficult to deal with an athletic culture whereby athletes expect that they will be able to participate in hazing initiations, and to continue a system that most seem genuinely to support.

> In the last situations that we dealt with, I interviewed some twenty student-athletes most of which were first-year. They were one-on-one interviews. All the first-year athletes thoroughly enjoyed the [hazing] experience, wouldn't want us to eliminate this, feel that it is a great way to get to know the team and to bond with the team and be accepted within the team. All of those things are very real in their lives, it is a real challenge for us across the universities and in sport in general to be able to implement change. To just come down with a heavy hand will just bury it and it will just continue underground. (A.D.)

This Athletic Director understands the culture that exists amongst athletes. There are coaches who see the initiation ceremony as a right to be exercised within their community. Sanctioning teams that violate policy can have the effect of driving the practice further away from any administrative means of detection. The A.D. feels that sanctions must be accompanied by programs that facilitate change within the community.

Alternative choices: Faced with the daunting task of overhauling a system steeped in tradition, the two Athletic Departments studied have attempted (one more than the other) to create viable and progressive alternatives to curtail the negative impacts of initiation. This includes several teams being involved in outdoor educational programs, and related activities such as ropes courses. Although successful on a small scale, these team-bonding alternatives still do not break the cycle of initiations that exists within the sport community:

> We have had some success. Some of our teams have gone to ropes courses, for example, men's and women's tennis were on a weekend ropes course. They have a very short season and they had the opportunity to look at a team building exercise like that. They found that to be really successful. We have other examples like that. We can look at ongoing education, every year we are going to be dealing with somebody who has a different belief system. We can look at giving alternatives to that kind of team building. The response that I am getting from some of the athletes is that unless it comes from the athletes themselves they will go through that team building really to comply with the regulations of the coach or the administration and then they go and do their own thing [initiation] anyway. It just goes way underground. The thing that I think we need to continue to focus in on is how do we deal with the situations where they are engaging in this kind of activity. All this education and alternatives is not going to bring us to the point where we are not going to be dealing with some kinds of problems. (A.D.)

There is an administrative understanding of the specific need to change the student-athlete's desire to pursue hazing as a means of constructing the concept of team and its accompanying identities. Accomplishing this, however, requires efforts to influence younger (pre-university) participants in sport culture and the "feeder systems" of the universities. Initiation is a seed that is planted and begins germinating long before the athlete reaches post-secondary education.

> One of the problems is that it is so prevalent in our feeder system that it is going to take a lot more to change it than a couple of workshops. "Jean Montague," who is quite active at another university, feels that twenty-four hours of intense activity is needed per team to have an impact. It is very much a challenge to all of us. I don't know

how practical it is for us to go into the education system and address this problem. In theory it is great. (A.D.)

However, there are examples from student-athletes of how alternative initiations have served to break the cycle of hazing within a team's culture:

This past year we went up to a camp for a weekend retreat where we were able to do ropes courses and canoe tripping. It was really an awesome weekend; we had been having trouble with the [Athletic] Department about our initiation, so this is what we did instead. I think that it worked on several different levels, the team really feels like a group this year. (Stephanie)

Teams are beginning to attempt alternative initiations as they are being made more readily available to them.

COACHES' PERSPECTIVES

A crucial part of the initiation ceremony is leadership. Prior to widespread public knowledge of initiation practices and direct administrative intervention, coaches often assumed an active role in the process. Coaches have become more ambivalent and distant during this period of change, primarily out of fear of administrative repercussions. There has been an attempt by some Athletic Departments to re-integrate their coaching staff into the transitional and orientation designs for their respective teams. This has been in reaction to the events which transpired in 1999. During that year, three teams were sanctioned by their university for hazing infractions. This was the first time that Ontario teams had been disciplined as a result of their initiations.

Knowledge and Understanding of the University Policy

Since coaches at the two universities studied are involved in meetings and seminars with the administration, they are made well aware of university and Athletic Department policies regarding hazing. Previously, when the acceptable parameters of hazing had not been established, there was ambiguity about the ramifications of such practices. However, it is now clearly understood that such practices are no longer acceptable in Athletic Departments:

> The policy is all laid out in the student code of conduct, it is new as of last year, and there were some suspensions in water polo. The policy has been in a state of evolution and they have been fine-tuning it. Prior to two years ago there was no clear definite policy. If there was it was not as finely detailed. The university never dealt with a hazing incident prior to this in any kind of organized way. (Coach)

Coaches were in a vulnerable position before Athletic Departments developed specific initiation policies :

> When word started getting out in the media about initiations and hazing, we started getting the message that this was not going to be tolerated anymore within our department. We weren't really sure what they were going to do, they weren't even sure what they were going to do to stop it, so I told my team that there wasn't going to be any more initiations. We really needed some kind of direction on this thing, I really think that it is useful, you know? But I shut it down, it wasn't worth losing the program. Even though I got out of it, I knew that it was still going on, someone would show up with a haircut or they would be really hungover. Saying stop didn't do it. (Coach)

Changing the Culture of Initiation

Athletic Departments are now taking initiatives in an attempt to change the pervasive initiation practices entrenched in their varsity culture. These include sanctions as well as educational seminars and alternative orientation experiences. Although some of these initiatives have been in place only a short while, there is some skepticism about their potential for effectiveness.

> I don't think that I would make any changes to the policy as it is now. I have never been a person who believes that penalties are deterrents, but we have tried for five years in many ways to try and bring policies to bear and we have shown them the videotapes. We showed that to our guys and to the executive and they are shaken up, they say how awful it is and then a week later they go to their own

"Rookie Night." There have been all kinds of efforts to stop it and nothing has worked so this year they actually decided to impose a penalty. We got caught and men's volleyball got caught. (Coach)

Stiff penalties will not be enough. There has to be something to fill the void left by not being able to initiate. I guess that is up to us. (Coach)

These coaches feel that strong administrative sanctions will not be enough to discourage and alter initiation practices, and that there needs to be an accompanying substitute for the more traditional forms of initiating.

Even in an environment where teams have suffered sanctions and forfeitures, and risk further suspensions, initiation continues to thrive:

The captain of our team that works in the neighborhood bar where everyone goes to says that the first three weeks of the term every team is parading through the bar. I think that it still goes on because honestly it is fun for the vast majority of people and a couple of people are likely traumatized by it and if they are they may say that they enjoyed it but secretly didn't, don't want to own up to it unless you have them in a room talking to them for three hours before they finally admit that part of it they weren't too keen about. I think that most people like that are ambivalent, they may have resented part of it but at the time thought that they were having a blast. So it is also possible to be the same person having mixed feelings about the same event. But it also has this strong cultural appeal and it's like sports violence, people love it. (Coach)

It would appear that changing the behaviours and attitudes associated with hazing initiations in the varsity culture will require more than heavy-handed administrative policy.

Role of the Coach

The role of the coach in a team's initiation practices is defined by the coaches themselves in accordance with the wishes of their Athletic Departments. They see themselves as the liaison between administrators and athletes for the dissemination of the information about their team's welcoming activities. However, despite the coach's good intentions, at times his or her message is misinterpreted:

> Once I found out what was going on, I was a bit miffed because I had
> to tell these guys not to do these things and pride myself at having a
> good communication level with the players, but none the less,
> behind my back they did it (initiated). I wonder sometimes whether
> they think that when I say "don't do it," they interpret that as I say
> don't do it because he has to say don't do it. But rather that I mean
> it is all right if I don't know about it. Which hasn't been the case at
> all because we cannot do this because we can be suspended. (Coach)

Some coaches will completely remove themselves from the process, in the
hope that the distance will not implicate them or their team:

> I told them not to do anything and prayed that they would listen to
> me, but there was also a part of me that wanted them to come up
> with something on their own because I knew that I couldn't be
> around for it. (Coach)

In addition, a few coaches have taken it upon themselves to establish progressive welcoming activities for their first-year players. Although these
individuals are rare, there are some preliminary indications that more
coaches are embracing some of these ideas:

> For the past few years, our team has been welcoming new members in
> a very positive inclusive fashion. We have been doing charity drives,
> scavenger hunts, a variety of alternative type of activities which attempt
> to integrate our team as opposed to structuring it in a hierarchy. The
> feedback has been really positive from the team. (Coach)

However, this type of involvement would not necessarily be a welcome
addition to the workload of some coaches:

> I like to think that I am a pretty progressive coach in a lot of ways, I
> am not authoritarian. But I also feel that I should be coaching the
> game and not coaching people how to live. I don't want to spend
> half of my life monitoring people's behaviour away from when I am
> actually with them. There is that aspect to it. I can't keep control of

them all of the time so if they happen to do stuff then I don't want it to come down on my shoulders. Which invariably it does. The first phone call is to me. I could see the benefit of the coach taking an active role in constructing or being a part of some kind of bonding ceremony. I am not thrilled about the idea of spending more time devoted to organizing that event, I am busy enough now. (Coach)

There is also an admission on the part of some coaches that their direct involvement could change the initiation behaviours of their teams:

If I were to get involved with the initiation ceremony, I know that I could bring it back to something that would suit all of us. The captains have been running the show for some time now and I have a feeling that it has been carried away at times. Sometimes it is better not to know. (Coach)

Coaches see their role as a crucial and viable part of the initiation ceremony, but for various reasons, largely in response to the moral panic and subsequent administrative policies, they have removed themselves from the process. For those who have remained, or have taken a new direction with activities designed to welcome new players, their involvement has been positive.

THE FUTURE OF INITIATIONS: WHAT THE ATHLETES SAY

Athletes in this study made many recommendations for changes to their respective varsity initiation practices. However, many of the respondents stated that, in all probability, their ceremonies would remain the same.

Alcohol Responsibility

There was an acknowledgment that greater responsibility should be taken by veteran players with regard to the consumption of alcohol, although this seems to be more a reaction to university hazing policy than a commitment to creating a more welcoming, inclusive environment.

I would want to keep it the way that we do it with our team, having a few guys stay sober to take care of the drunken rookies. There is a responsibility, there has to be a series of checks and balances. Sober drivers, someone in control, we are just more prepared now. It used to be that we were all drunk and you don't notice the really drunk ones when you yourself are in that state. That is when you run into troubles. (Paulo)

Even if this is in response to university policy, to a certain degree it will control the rookies' alcohol use and offer some protection in the area where most hazing-related problems occur.

Alternative Initiations

The participants offered various suggestions for alternative initiations: team parties, road trips, team meal preparations, training camps, meals at the coach's or a team member's house, retreats to cabins, canoe trips, barbecues, movies, videos, rope courses, and scavenger hunts. All of the recommendations were far removed from activities in which participants had been previously involved, seeming to suggest that there is a need to replace tradition with new directions and activities. Events that are rich in egalitarian and democratic principles, that reduce competition or involve competition in a form that puts both veterans and rookies on an equal footing, that level the playing field and remove the power-based structure that is an ever-present component of initiations—all of these were considered to be valuable alternatives.

It is almost better to do an activity that is not your sport. Take canoe tripping for example, most people haven't done something like that. So everyone is on the same playing field, it doesn't have the built-in hierarchy where power can be, there is an imbalance of power. Take them out of their element and have them do something that is totally unique. (Mark)

At least some athletes appear to feel that alternative initiations could be of value.

Superficial Changes

Some cosmetic changes were suggested. They included changing the name of the ceremony from initiation or hazing to "party" or some other phrase, primarily as an attempt to remove the negative connotations that surround the former titles. Another suggestion, coming from a participant whose team holds initiation ceremonies at the end of their season, was to change the timing to the beginning of the year. A reverse initiation, which is when the rookies initiate the veteran players as opposed to the traditional sequence, was also recommended, the theory being that it would be centered on fun and partying as opposed to payback.

Administration Involvement

One suggestion was to involve the athletic administration, financially and organizationally, in team initiations. There was a call for more direction and guidance to support alternative team activities, especially in times of fiscal constraint.

> My suggestion was to give them some direction, give them a rookie package, and throw them a welcoming party. I would love to have a laser tag day or go-cart day because that is fun. Going somewhere that is not your sport, because you do that every day. Something that doesn't necessarily involve alcohol, but the problem is organizing it. Especially with such a short season. To get a bus, to fundraise. Honestly, it is just easier to put on candy necklaces and go to the bar. I would like to see the school put forward some of the money to set up these initiation programs. (Tanja)

This comment pinpoints funding as one of the reasons that the cheaper, traditional types of initiations are utilized. Greater financial commitment on the part of Athletic Departments could facilitate the transition to alternative types of activities.

Coaches' Involvement

When traditional initiations ceased to be acceptable in the eyes of the public, coaches started to distance themselves from the process. When universities starting drafting anti-hazing policies, intended to curtail this behaviour, most coaches adopted a "don't ask, don't tell" attitude. Effectively left on their own, captains and team leaders assumed responsibility for the construction and implementation of the initiation ceremonies.

However, several of the respondents suggested that they would like to see their coaches once again involved in the process:

> I think that the initiation would be better if the coach was there, they know it goes on, but I think that they can't let on because they are afraid they might get in trouble, that is my take anyway. It makes sense, they make the decisions about our team, why not about the initiation? (Sean)

The athletes apparently wish to have the coaches reinvolved in the transitional process.

Resistance to Change

In contrast to these suggestions is the reality that some of the teams do not want to change any of their initiation practices.

> I wouldn't change anything because I think that it is cool and it works for us. (Paulo)

There is a strong resistance from players, from coaches, even within administrations, to any sort of directed change in initiation practices. Most of the respondents who wanted to see no change in future initiation practices were male. One captain speculated about the response of teams were they to be presented with initiation alternatives:

> Probably the backlash will come from teams like the men's rugby or water polo teams, because if they can't put the money towards kegs they will think that it is wussy. Why will we do that? Maybe it is a gender thing too, if you have all of the girls saying yes, let's do that and you would have the guys saying no way, that is dumb. Who is to say that you couldn't do both and then one may transform into the better of each. Maybe you go out for beers after laser tag. Make it a full-day event. You get more bonding out of that. (Jenn)

The teams in Athletic Departments that have attempted alternative orientations have, for the most part, been female.

CONCLUSION

Universities have been forced to take an active role over the last five or six years in response to the moral outcry concerning orientation, initiation, and hazing practices at their institutions. In large part they have developed policies intended to protect the university's interests in the case of any potential lawsuits. Although some university administrations are offering specific alternatives and directives to their membership, most university policies outline what cannot take place, but present no guidance or information on viable alternatives. Most universities had no policies in place until the media started covering the issue, and the practices began to be condemned in a public forum. When the issue of university athletic hazing came to light in the latter half of the 1990s, university administrators were essentially forced into action.

However, the data presented in this chapter suggests that coaches, players, and athletic directors recognize that anti-hazing policies on their own are not enough to deter hazing behaviours. On the other hand, there seems to be a widespread belief that a strong policy, with real sanctions for infractions, and an educational component with alternative orientations that enable teams to retain the ritual of welcoming new members into the community in a positive and inclusive fashion, can facilitate constructive team bonding and interaction and can indeed shift the hazing paradigm in a new direction.

REFERENCES

Bryshun, J. (1997). *Hazing in sport: An exploratory study of veteran/rookie relations.* Unpublished Master's thesis, University of Calgary, Calgary, Alberta.

Curtis, M. (1996). "The transition and orientation experiences of first-year athletes at the University of Toronto," in *Draft of an evaluation project conducted by the Office of Student Affairs.*

Fifth estate. (October 29, 1996). *Thin ice.* Canadian Broadcasting Corporation.

Johnson, J. (2000). *Sport hazing experiences in the context of anti-hazing policies— The case of two Southern Ontario universities.* Unpublished Master's thesis, University of Toronto.

Robinson, L. (1998). *Crossing the line: Violence and sexual assault in Canada's national sport.* Toronto: McClelland and Stewart Inc.

CHAPTER 10

Changing the Initiation Ceremony

Jay Johnson and Patricia Miller

Victims of hazing incidents have reported enduring a host of vulgarities. Abuses have included verbal, physical and sexual assault, sometimes repeated and often quite horrific (Johnson, 2000; Nuwer, 1999). The consequences have included mild to severe physical injuries; intense emotional and psychological distress; difficulty sleeping, eating and concentrating; low self-esteem; poor academic performance; post-traumatic stress disorder; and altercations with police, leading for some to criminal convictions (Nuwer, 1999). More alarming, researchers have reported that young men and women die each year as a result of hazing incidents (Nuwer, 1999). These are the extreme cases, but their occurrence is sobering and the impact of the deaths of these young people on their families, friends and communities devastating.

Despite these serious, sometimes lethal consequences, hazing exists in diverse settings in high numbers. Initiation incidents have been reported in the military, in police and fire departments, in fraternities and sororities, and across college campuses in a host of other student organizations. Investigators estimate that 48% of high-school students are subjected to "questionable" or "unacceptable" initiation practices.

Initiation rituals also have long traditions in the sport culture. Initiations on professional, university, club, and even high-school athletic teams have been exposed in recent years (Bryshun, 1997; Johnson, 2000; Robinson, 1998). For example, hazing incidents have been publicly reported involving the University of Vermont's men's hockey team, Brock University's men's rugby team, as well as the rugby teams at the University of New Brunswick and McMaster University, and the University of Western Ontario's football team.

There are a number of possible explanations for the long existence of hazing rituals in sport subcultures. Some might argue initiation activities are fun and exciting. Others suggest athletes succumb to peer pressure and just go along with their teammates. Some athletes may feel participating in hazing is a way to prove their strength and courage to their peers, or their unwavering commitment to their teams.

Those who support initiation ceremonies insist hazing rituals ultimately serve to bond new and existing team members into a cohesive group. In exchange for enduring "rookie nights," newcomers receive the right to affiliation with and membership on the team. It is often under this guise of bonding and cohesion that initiations endure.

The desire to feel connected to and a part of a group is understandable, particularly for those in new, unfamiliar environments. Yet, the belief that hazing leads to feelings of belonging and membership is flawed. Athletes, and fraternity and sorority pledges have reported feeling angry, embarrassed, guilty and humiliated as a result of hazing incidents, and some have chosen to leave the teams and organizations they so desperately wanted to be a part of in the first place (Johnson, 2000). Furthermore, the available research on initiations suggests hazing establishes and perpetuates a formidable power imbalance between veterans and rookies rather than feelings of belonging and equity (Messner and Sabo, 1994).

Despite the prevalence of initiations in the sport culture, there is a discernible concern among athletes about the risks and consequences of hazing rituals. Johnson (2000), who interviewed current and former male and female university student-athletes about hazing in the university sport culture, found athletes had begun to question abusive hazing traditions on their teams. Indeed, many had started to reconsider the value of such activities and their apparently innocuous nature. Johnson suggested student-athletes were poised for change, yet he recognized that they were often at a loss about how to stop long-held hazing traditions.

A number of suggestions are available. Indeed, several strategies have emerged already, each achieving some measure of success. One of the strategies for which parents, educators and other activists have lobbied heavily has been anti-hazing legislation (Nuwer, 1999). Consequently, most states in the U.S. have adopted strict anti-hazing laws over the last ten years. Similarly, many individual organizations and institutions across North America have implemented either hazing policies or codes of conduct that include anti-hazing regulations. Finally, some anti-hazing activists have developed educational programs and tour widely, speaking at high schools and universities about the dangers of hazing rituals (Nuwer, 1999).

Another viable approach to help end abusive, demoralizing hazing is to substitute alternative welcoming orientation experiences for existing hazing traditions in sport subcultures. This approach, introduced in isolated areas and well received by the student-athletes involved, is slightly different than those listed above. It attempts not to eliminate orientation events, but to change their nature. While hazing scenarios have not traditionally done so, alternative orientation activities can reflect the principles of inclusivity, respect, and freedom of choice, and should occur in non-threatening environments characterized by shared power and decision-making. We have compiled a list of alternative orientation activities to help coaches, team leaders, and returning players welcome new players in an open atmosphere free of the discrimination, segregation, and degradation that typically characterize hazing rituals.

In each case, we have provided ways in which the activity/experience could be adapted based on financial or resource limitations, time restrictions, and/or size of team. We have also made important cautionary notes where applicable. Several of the orientation experiences included herein involve activities that, if poorly planned or insufficiently supervised, could lead to accidents or injuries.

First, however, we would like to offer some general guidelines regarding the introduction of alternative, welcoming orientation activities.

The effort to replace abusive, often dangerous, hazing ceremonies with welcoming orientation activities will require coordinated input from multiple groups including coaches, athletes, alumni, support staff, administrators, officials, parents and relatives, and where applicable, athletic directors, school administrators, teachers/faculty, and student service personnel. It is critical that athletes, new and returning, be included in this process. If athletes are invited to play an integral role in designing and promoting alternative transition experiences, they will be more likely to adopt and endorse these new traditions on their teams.

The effort to stop hazing must be a sustained one. Many of the initiation rites on sports teams have long histories and are ritualistically passed from one cohort to the next. It will be difficult to break such traditions, but not impossible. Some Greek organizations have been successful in changing the nature of their pledge activities, despite daunting barriers and recurring setbacks (Nuwer, 1999).

Orientation experts argue that the first six weeks in a new environment are a critical period for newcomers. It is during this period that newcomers are most likely to develop feelings of belonging and familiarity. We therefore recommend that transition experiences for athletes be offered during the first six weeks of the athletic season.

Alcohol plays an insidious role in hazings and initiations, particularly those that take place on college and university campuses. A survey of 325,000 athletes from more than 1,000 NCAA schools revealed that more than half were subjected to alcohol-related initiations, including being forced to consume large amounts of alcohol at a single time, to drink to the point of passing out, to participate in drinking contests, and to ingest disgusting concoctions of alcohol.

Alcohol has also been implicated in numerous deaths following initiation ceremonies on university campuses. Eigen (1994) reported that 90% of hazing deaths on U.S. college campuses involved alcohol.

Some institutions have responded to the prevalence of drinking by undergraduate students, and its implication in hazing practices, by banning alcohol altogether on their campuses (Nuwer, 1999). Often, this has forced drinking underground or off-campus. Other institutions have adopted the position that the majority of students are underage, and by definition, should not be drinking, thus absolving themselves of further responsibility.

The reality is that many students do drink. Alcohol consumption on college and university campuses in North America is widespread. Some believe it has become epidemic, that our undergraduates habitually consume staggering amounts of alcohol. Investigators have found 45% of male and 35% of female college students are binge drinkers (Riordan and Dane, 1998). These numbers soared to 86% and 80% for men and women, respectively, involved in Greek organizations. To ignore the prevalence of drinking on campus and the abuse of alcohol in initiations and hazings among the college culture is a grave mistake, a missed opportunity to educate students about alcohol and drug abuse. In the words of Riordan and Dane (1998), "[i]nstitutions that prohibit alcohol entirely miss the opportunity to help students learn to make responsible choices" (53). Educational programs, intervention and counselling programs, close supervision and scrutiny of student activities, clearly defined policies and penalties for violations, are some ways in which universities can begin to address alcohol use by student-athletes in hazing rituals.

The available research suggests initiations and hazings commonly involve sexual abuse and degradation (Bryshun and Young, 1999; Johnson, 2000; Holman, 1997). The NCAA study mentioned above found both male and female student-athletes were forced to tell or listen to dirty jokes, undress, or appear nude in public, dress provocatively or as a member of the opposite sex (Hoover, 1999). More serious sexual abuse has been reported, including being molested by teammates or members of other teams, being forced to perform oral sex on others, being raped and gang-raped or being expected to participate in these acts. Sexually explicit initiations may be more prevalent on co-ed teams, or in sports that offer both a men's and a women's team. We recommend that all activities of a sexual nature be banned from welcoming orientation activities, even those that appear benign or harmless. To counter that athletes often consent to participate in sexualized hazing incidents fails to recognize that it is impossible to distinguish between consent given freely and consent given under duress, under the influence of alcohol, or as a perceived condition of acceptance.

If they have not yet done so, sport organizations and educational institutions should establish clear and specific anti-hazing policies and sanctions, and disseminate this information to athletes, coaches, athletic directors, and other athletics personnel, parents, and alumni. Furthermore, sport organizations and educational institutions must uniformly enforce sanctions against individuals and teams who persist in carrying out inappropriate initiation rituals regardless of the possible damage to an athletic program or institution's reputation.

The objective of orientation activities is to introduce new members to all of the people and resources in their new environment. Orientation events should include athletes from different teams, as well as coaching and support staff, administrative personnel, and individuals from other athlete support services.

Below are eight alternative orientation activities that incorporate these recommendations and are intended to serve either as complete orientation events or as the skeletons for your own welcoming activities.

ACTIVITY 1: ROPES AND CHALLENGE COURSE

Ropes and challenge courses have gained significant popularity in the last decade. Ropes and challenge courses include a series of natural and artificial obstacles in outdoor settings designed to encourage participants to move beyond their personal boundaries. Exposure to activities is typically followed by group debriefing during which group leaders or facilitators prompt participants to explore the personal meaning of the experience and its relevance to their professional and personal lives.

These activities are used for numerous purposes among diverse groups. They have, for example, been effective in increasing the risk-taking of male fire fighters (MacRae et al., 1998) and the cohesion among co-workers from both government and corporate settings (Daniels, 1994; Priest and Lesperance, 1994). Ropes and challenge courses are also used regularly by groups such as Project Adventure and Outward Bound to increase the communication and leadership skills of youth and young adults.

Ropes and challenge courses have also emerged in sport settings, primarily as a tool to promote cohesion. In fact, early research suggests these adventure activities can effectively increase team cohesion, as well as generate other positive changes. Meyer and Wenger (1998) reported that members of a girls' high-school tennis team who voluntarily participated in a one-day ropes and challenge course experienced increased self-confidence, concentration, awareness of teammates, trust among teammates, and improved commitment and dedication to the team.

The ability of ropes and challenge courses to effect team cohesion is important to our discussion of alternative orientation experiences. Miller (2000) introduced the idea of using ropes and challenge courses as an alternative to traditional hazing practices in the fall of 1999 at the University of Toronto. Acting as consultants to the athletics department, Miller, in collaboration with a colleague, Johnson, organized a weekend retreat for seven male and female university teams at a ropes and challenge facility. Athletes and coaches participated in low and high ropes elements, trust activities, and several initiatives in team and mixed groups. Anecdotal accounts from participants were positive and revealed the experience provided athletes with opportunities to get to know each other, as well as athletes from other teams. New players enjoyed getting to know their peers and coaches in a non-sport setting, and returning players admitted they learned new things about teammates they had known, in some cases, for several years. Although empirical research is needed, these initial accounts suggest ropes and challenge courses are a viable alternative to abusive hazing ceremonies.

Those interested in this option should consult their local directories for facilities in their area. Facilities can typically accommodate weekend or day activities, and regularly charge a standard per person rate. Group rates may be available. No certification or licensing agency currently oversees ropes and challenge courses in Canada or the U.S.A. One should ask about the training and experience of facilitators, including their familiarity with the debriefing process; the age, stability, and choice of low and high ropes elements; and the available of safety equipment such as helmets and harnesses. It is important to ensure there is a safe facilitator-participant ratio, and that safety procedures and policies are clearly articulated upon arrival.

A visit to a ropes and challenge course should take place shortly after team selection, and special attention should be paid to the family, academic, work, and spiritual obligations of team members. Coaches and other support staff should, whenever possible, participate in these activities, and new and returning players should be paired together.

The cost of a ropes and challenge course may be prohibitive for some teams. An alternative would be to learn about some of the trust/spotting activities, as well as some of the initiatives that do not require special equipment or facilities. Several of these are described below.

Crossing the Nile: Students can be provided with a number of planks, boxes, or rises and ropes of different lengths in an open space, such as a gym or field. The group must cross from Point A to Point B, using only the objects provided, without having any part of their body touch the ground/floor.

Guiding Hands: Divide team members into smaller groups of three or four. Blindfold one individual in the group while the other three navigate him/her across an obstacle course designed by members of the group, without any form of verbal communication. Alternatively, the group could be assigned to teach the blindfolded member a simple body movement routine, again without any form of verbal communication.

High Voltage: Tie ropes at different heights around three or four trees or poles, creating an enclosed space protected by an "electronic barrier" below the ropes. The objective of this exercise is to get all team members out of the enclosed area, without being electrified.

Circle of Friends/Wave: One individual stands in the centre with team-mates surrounding him/her. When the individual is ready, he/she allows him/herself to fall forward or backward into the teammates' waiting hands.

ACTIVITY 2: COMMUNITY SERVICE PROJECT

Several years ago, the women's volleyball team at the University of Toronto pooled together their money, purchased the necessary ingredients, and, at the family restaurant of one of the players, prepared a Christmas meal for a local shelter. Team members and coaches divided tasks throughout the day, often working in small groups, allowing players and coaches to work together in a non-sport setting. Team members then delivered the meal to the shelter, along with other needed items they had collected, including clothing, children's toys, bedding, and kitchenware. Team members felt very positive about helping others in need and about getting to know each other in new capacities.

Each year, students at Carleton University in Ottawa coordinate a one-day shoe shine charity fund-raiser. Students are paired together and assigned a location in the corporate sector of the city where they offer shoe shines in exchange for a donation. Proceeds are forwarded to a charity of choice, often the Children's Hospital.

Community service projects such as these are often undertaken at times of special need (Thanksgiving, Christmas, Easter). We would like to suggest such projects could be used as orientation activities. One of the advantages of this transitional experience is that many people, including youth and young adults, have volunteer experience and can bring some measure of expertise to community service projects, a dynamic that may avert power imbalances and instead foster acceptance and friendship among teammates.

Present the idea at one of the first team meetings of the season and have players generate a list of possible community-service projects. Select one as a group, one consistent with the mission of the athletic program or organization and perhaps of personal significance to a player, coach, or support staff. Community service projects could include a food or clothing drive for a local shelter, a day or more extensive volunteer commitment to a local organization, a skills workshop or sports camp for local children or community center, a fund-raising event for a local or national charity. There are an infinite number of ways to raise money for charitable causes: lotteries, raffles, 50-50 draws, fashion shows, golf or other sports tournaments, car washes, bake sales, plant sales, exam care package sales.

If players are uncertain of the immediate needs of their community, have them consult a volunteer organization, the local volunteer bureau, or the blue pages of their local directory.

Once a community service project has been determined, have team members compile a task list of duties, divide the items among pairs of new and returning players, establish deadlines, and schedule follow-up meetings.

You may wish to alternate community projects from year to year, or retain the same one over the years. The objective is to establish a new, prosocial tradition that encourages players to collaborate as equals on a meaningful project.

If there are too few members on your team to successfully complete a community service project in the early season without interfering with athletic, academic or work schedules, cooperate with another team or organization. Perhaps invite alumni to continue their involvement by participating in the project.

If there are too many members on your team to make working together on a single project impractical, as may be the case with a football or track and field team, divide players into smaller groups, being sure to intermingle new and returning players and players who might not otherwise have a great deal of interaction, and have each group work on a separate community project. Alternatively, the team as a whole could select a charity, and subgroups work on different fund-raising events, competing with one another to see who can raise the most money or in the most creative way, in the least amount of time, etc. One word of caution: the intention is to create a welcoming environment for all players and competition between groups should be good-natured and tempered by the overall goal of the orientation experience.

One more cautionary note: the nature of working groups suggests there will be group members who work hard and others who do not. Coaches or team leaders must ensure responsibilities are divided equally and not heaped on new members, particularly as they adjust to their new surroundings and the demands of their new positions.

ACTIVITY 3: BIG BROTHER–LITTLE BROTHER/ BIG SISTER–LITTLE SISTER MENTORING

New team members will likely bond with one another by virtue of their shared status as newcomers. The relationships between new and existing team members, however, can be tenuous. Traditional hazing ceremonies that pit veterans against rookies serve only to exacerbate this dynamic.

Coaches and student leaders must strive to eliminate these skewed power relations. One way in which to create a more equitable environment is to introduce a big brother–little brother/big sister–little sister mentoring system. In this scenario, each new player is paired with a senior or returning player who is responsible for welcoming the new player and protecting him/her from harm. New and senior players could be paired randomly, although it may be more effective to ensure the two share something in common other than their sport.

The mentoring literature suggests mentors serve two primary functions: psychosocial and supportive (Davidson, 2001; Neill and Heubeck, 1998). In a high school, college, or university setting, the senior athlete could provide support in both the athletic and academic settings. In the athletic environment, the senior player could introduce his/her protégé to team rules, both formal and informal, familiarize him or her with facilities and important personnel (athletic director, program coordinator, athletic training staff, sport psychology staff), and model skills and drills in practice. The two could also travel and room together on road trips. In the academic setting, the veteran could provide information about course selection, course registration, important deadlines and personnel (registrar, dean/chair, academic advisor, tutor, coordinator of support services for student-athletes).

Mentors and protégés could be alternated through the season, ensuring new players have the occasion to work with several senior players.

Formal mentoring relationships may be unfamiliar in some environments, particularly those where seniors have a history of enjoying preferred status and have little interaction with incoming players, other than through hazing rituals. If this is the case, veterans would benefit from a discussion about the intent of the mentoring system, how to create an open, accepting atmosphere, and how to avoid traditional hazing rituals and the power imbalances they engender. Coaches may also wish to establish guidelines defining acceptable and unacceptable behaviour for mentors and protégés.

Should participation in a formal mentoring relationship be mandatory? What if, for example, a senior does not want to mentor a new player? Or, if a new player does not wish to spend time with a mentor? While this will ultimately be a decision for coaches, players forced to participate in a mentoring relationship are unlikely to benefit from the experience. Coaches are cautioned against making participation in a mentoring system mandatory.

ACTIVITY 4: RELAY SCAVENGER HUNT

This suggestion is based on an actual orientation activity organized for new members of a university figure skating team. The objective of the activity was to challenge team members to collaborate with one another and build team unity through a relay scavenger hunt.

The team was divided into small groups of new and returning players. Each group was given an envelope containing a different question. An example may have been, "What are the office hours of the Dean of Arts and Sciences?" To answer the question, the group had to proceed to the office of the Dean of Arts and Sciences and ask, whereupon they received a second envelope containing another question. Each group completed a handful of questions, all regarding personnel (e.g., athletic director, sports medicine physician, athletic therapist, sport psychology consultant, equity officer, academic advisor), programs (e.g., leadership development office, work study program), or services (e.g., financial aid, counseling services, career services) of particular interest to incoming student-athletes. All groups received a final riddle, the solution to which was the location of a special meeting with a surprise guest, an Olympic skater.

Notably, this activity took place in a single afternoon and required few resources other than creativity. It could be adapted in several ways. Instead of receiving the questions at different locations, the groups could be given a list of questions at the outset. The event could be timed and the quickest group rewarded. New players could generate lists of questions based on what they would like to learn, and then the list passed on to a different group. Senior members could be asked to develop questions based on things they wish they had known when they joined the team, and these lists traded among the groups.

Scavenger hunts have a tainted history, in large part because lists traditionally included items that had to be stolen: street signs, restaurant or bar paraphernalia, personal belongings. Bonus points were often awarded for the most difficult or risky-to-retrieve items. However, we believe if used in the manner described above—to collect helpful information, increase the familiarity of incoming players with their new surroundings, and give new and returning players the opportunity to interact in non-sport settings— scavenger hunts can be a viable and beneficial orientation activity.

ACTIVITY 5: SIGHT-SEEING TOUR

Moving to a new city can be a daunting experience. It may be particularly so for young athletes who know no one in their new community and are away from home for the first time. Elsewhere we have provided suggestions to orient new players to their teams and immediate athletic facilities. It might also be helpful to orient incoming athletes to their local communities. A sightseeing tour can be an innovative way to welcome new team members and to allow new and existing team members to bond.

To avoid travel difficulties, consider a walking tour or a tour by public transit. The whole team could travel together or break up into small groups, ensuring new team members are paired with senior or returning players. Include popular tourist destinations on the tour, as well as places that may be of particular interest or use to new members. For university student-athletes, this might include the local laundromat, bank, movie theatre, grocery store, photocopy service, used bookstore. Have returning players vote on a "best of" list (best pizza place, best breakfast place, best vegetarian restaurant, best magazine store, best music store, etc.) and show these spots to new players. A letter could be sent to incoming players asking them to identify places about which they would be especially interested in learning: local church or synagogue, local bike store, nearest skate boarding facility, best golf course in the area, closest rock-climbing facility. It might also be helpful to highlight areas or places new players would wish to avoid: a dangerous neighbourhood, a parking lot that is poorly lit at night, a terrible restaurant.

There are a number of advantages to this activity. It is inexpensive and could be completed in a short amount of time. It takes advantage of the experiences of existing players and demonstrates a concern for both the transition and interests of new players. It also provides an opportunity for new and existing players to interact in a non-sport setting.

ACTIVITY 6: SHARING A MEAL

Many groups have limited time for orientation activities. In the sport setting, there is often very little time between final team selection and the start of a full schedule of training, practices, travel, and games. The following is an activity that can be organized without a great deal of difficulty and completed within the span of a few hours, and if planned well, can include all new and returning players.

Groups regularly share meals together, in between long meetings, as a reward for reaching an important bench mark, at the completion of a challenging project, or to mark the departure of an important member of the group. Our suggestion is for a new group to share a meal at one of their first encounters. The meal could be breakfast, lunch, or dinner.

Attention to several matters will increase the likelihood of creating an open, accepting environment for new and existing team members. First, ensure everyone is introduced to one another. This can be done by simply going around the room and having each member share basic personal information (e.g., name, hometown, role on team). Alternatively, group members could split up into pairs or groups of three for several minutes, and then introduce each other to the larger group based on what they have learned about one another in the previous few minutes. Or, the group leader could ask each group member to confide a funny story or interesting item about him/herself and then share it with the group without identifying its source. Individuals or pairs of players could try to guess to whom each story/item belonged. After everyone has guessed, each member could then claim his/her story/item, sharing a more detailed account.

Second, ensure that every group member is able to attend and none is left out or without a means of getting to the meal.

Third, many people have limitations on the food they can or choose to eat for financial, religious, medical or other personal reasons. If dining out, ensure the menu will accommodate all group members. If uncertain, ask group members about preferences beforehand.

Dining out can sometimes be costly, particularly for students, and taking a large group to breakfast, lunch, or dinner could be prohibitive for teams operating on a small budget. An alternative is to organize a pot luck. Pairs of new and returning players could be assigned one course of the meal, then shop and cook together. Teams whose members come from diverse backgrounds could be invited to bring a dish native to their birthplace. Group leaders must ensure that new group members are not pressured or forced into bringing all or the most expensive items or, if eating out, paying the bill.

There are countless variations to this theme: a chili cook-off, a barbecue, a cookie exchange. The important features are that all group members have the opportunity to interact, none is left out, and no one subgroup is given greater or all of the organizational or financial responsibilities for the meal.

ACTIVITY 7: OUTDOOR RECREATION ACTIVITY

A wealth of literature examines the phenomenon of outdoor recreation as a form of orientation, particularly with first-year university students. The studies reveal a variety of applications and benefits including academic gains, integration into the scholastic setting, and improved retention rates (Davidson, 2001; Hastie,1995; Hattie et al., 1997).

Outdoor recreation activities include a range of experiences, several of which are described below. Each, when used as an orientation strategy, is intended to involve all team members in a welcoming, open atmosphere. As a cautionary note, it is advised that these activities be selected only if trained personnel are available to lead them and provide assistance.

Canoe/Hiking/Camping Excursion: The first suggestion would be a two to four day canoe trip. Most national parks offer hiking and canoeing trails, often sorted by difficulty and length. Group members should start by generating a list of responsibilities (e.g., arranging travel, organizing equipment, purchasing and packing meals, food preparation, and site planning) and dividing these among pairs or small groups of new and returning players. New and returning players should be grouped together in canoes, and group members rotated throughout the adventure to ensure each new member has the opportunity to meet returning players. Every canoe group should have the opportunity to lead the entire group (orienteering utilizing a compass and map) for a specific duration.

Orienteering: If time and/or equipment make the canoe/hiking trip impossible, an afternoon of outdoor activities could be organized. Team members are transported to a nearby park or conservation area where they are subdivided into smaller groups of three or four. Each small group is then dropped off at different starting points, and then, with only a compass, map, and lunch, attempts to rendezvous with the entire group at a final location at a specified time.

Indoor/Outdoor Rock Climbing: Indoor and outdoor rock-climbing facilities are available in most major cities. A group could spend a challenging and exciting day scaling and rappelling. Both individual and team activities could be organized at the facilities, and the process of challenging oneself and providing direction and encouragement to teammates would nurture team bonding.

ACTIVITY 8: SPORT RELATED ACTIVITY

The University of Toronto Varsity Tennis Team suggested a novel orientation experience for new students which involved organizing tennis clinics for young tennis enthusiasts based on recent changes in teaching methods and tennis skill development. The team proposed visiting local schools and spending about half an hour with students in grades one, two, and three, preferably during their scheduled gym class. The half-hour session included a warm-up, instruction, application through children's tennis games, and a cool-down period. The group's objective was to promote the sport of tennis at young age levels and the University of Toronto children's athletic programs. The team anticipated that the commitment of each team member to the project and time spent together in collaborative work would enhance team camaraderie and support systems.

If the idea of a sport-related orientation is appealing, the above example could be adapted in several ways. You could run a sports camp for a smaller group or a shorter time period, perhaps at a local community center or school. Alternatively, you could enter a recreational charity event as a team. Such events need not involve your sport. It is the opportunity to play together in a sport atmosphere that may facilitate new players' transition to their new environment.

Another experience might be to attend a high-profile training session or competition in your sport, e.g., an NBA or NHL game, an international volleyball or tennis tournament. This allows team members to draw upon the one thing they have in common while establishing relationships and friendships.

Teams are often limited by time and/or financial resources. Coaches and team leaders may consider introducing an orientation activity directly in practice or training sessions. A lot of teams begin their seasons with light or fun practices. To make this even more enjoyable for the players and to provide new players with an opportunity to demonstrate their skills and get to know their new teammates, alternate the traditional scrimmage rules. Implement an "All Touch" rule where every team member on one side has to touch the ball/puck before a team member can attempt scoring a point(s). Or, change the scoring system to a reverse order score, so the team who is scored against gets the points as opposed to the scoring team. Introduce a rotating player system, so that each time a player earns points, they rotate to the other team.

CONCLUSIONS AND FUTURE DIRECTIONS

We now know that hazing and initiation rituals are a component of teams at the high school, community, club, and college levels (Bryshun, 1997; Bryshun and Young, 1999; Holman, 1997; Hoover, 1999; Johnson, 2000, 2002; Robinson, 1998). We have also learned that hazing incidents are common in other subcultures, including other groups found in high schools and universities such as fraternities, sororities, and campus clubs, and in a wide range of professions.

We recognize that such activities are often intended to increase a sense of belonging, to augment group cohesion and bonding between group members, rather than to alienate and degrade newcomers. Unfortunately, however, the latter is a common outcome. Studies have found that initiation rituals frequently involve forced alcohol consumption, degradation and humiliation of the participants, as well as physical and sexual abuse (Bryshun, 1997; Bryshun and Young, 1999; Hoover and Pollard, 2000; Johnson, 2000, 2002; Meyer, 2000; Nuwer, 1999).

Change within the sport environment, a culture that almost by definition is rooted in long-standing traditions, will be difficult. New ideas are often greeted with resistance and skepticism, and produce a sluggish and petulant reform process. Change, however, is possible. Student-athletes have already voiced a desire to reconsider the need for and nature of abusive hazing practices.

Change will come about from a unified and comprehensive effort. Educational programs and other information-based interventions will provide much-needed knowledge about the risks and outcomes of traditional hazing rituals. Anti-hazing laws and institutional policies will offer a second layer of incentive for change, particularly when incidents are consistently investigated and harsh penalties imposed. The position we have presented here is that a library of welcoming orientation activities will provide direction to administrators, coaches, and athletes interested in introducing new traditions on their teams.

Further, we have argued that it is crucial to create activities that are attractive and exciting, and that can be seen as *real* alternatives to traditional hazing practices. Replacing existing hazing practices with clichéd or immature team-building activities is likely to encourage initiation leaders to take their activities underground and further hinder reform.

We believe the scenarios presented in this chapter are viable, attractive orientation activities. They maintain the bonding element so urgently sought in traditional hazing events, without the brutal and derisory methods and effects. They also model a structure that empowers senior and incoming athletes and gives them ownership of the newly constructed rituals surrounding team orientations.

The alternatives given in this chapter—community service projects, Big Brother–Little Brother/Big Sister–Little Sister mentoring, sightseeing tours, shared meals, outdoor recreation activities, sport related activities, high and low ropes courses, and scavenger hunts—are intended only as guides, and skeletons. Coaches and team leaders are advised to mold them to meet the unique needs of their teams. Administrators and program officials are encouraged, as much as possible, to support such activities through access to facilities, equipment, expertise, and funding. Doing so will send a critical message to all those involved about the importance of ending abusive hazing practices and creating new, welcoming experiences.

GLOSSARY

Sport Subcultures: Cultures or groups that, within the context of sport, operate with distinct habits, patterns, and rituals to distinguish their allegiance to each other separate from the "norm."

Ritual: Rituals involve sets of formally patterned behaviour, which are repeated at intervals of varying length, depending on the type of occasion. When people in a particular group engage in ritual behaviour, they transmit information to themselves and to each other about their current state of being. The information that people communicate in rituals is often a symbolic duplication and restatement of beliefs and social relationships within the group.

Alternative Orientation: Orientation ceremonies which are welcoming to all, de-emphasizing difference and separation and focusing on inclusivity, equality, and equity. Different from traditional initiation ceremonies which can be degrading, humiliating, and abusive for new members.

Mentoring: The process of acting as a guide, educator, and liaison for a newer member within a recognized institutional setting. The partnering of an experienced athlete with one who is newer to the team.

Rookie/Neophyte: A first-year player on a sports team is referred to as a rookie who, at the varsity level, can be any age.

Initiation or Hazing: "Hazing is defined as any action taken or situation created by an individual or group, intentionally or unintentionally, whether on or off college or university premises, to produce mental or physical discomfort, embarrassment, harassment, ridicule, or in any way demeans the dignity of another human being. Initiations, however explained, or activities that imply, encourage, condone, or allow students to misuse alcohol or other drugs, violate the law, or commit unethical, immoral or inappropriate behaviour are explicitly forbidden" (*University of Western Ontario student athlete handbook*: 18).

The initiation or hazing is the actual process involving the initiators and those being initiated. It is the ceremony whereby the individuals being initiated into the society perform the act.

> Any activity expected of someone joining a group that humiliates, degrades, abuses or endangers, regardless of the person's willingness to participate. This does not include activities such as rookies carrying the balls, team parties with community games, or going out with your teammates, unless an atmosphere of humiliation, degradation, abuse or danger arise. (Hoover, 1999, Appendix 111)

> The diminishing of other human beings through the use of insults, inferiorizing, and subservience are intended as a form of intimidation that coerces others to accept the autocracy and inequality of the structure, in this case, sport. (Holman, 1997: 2)

REFERENCES

Bryshun, J. (1997). *Hazing in sport: An exploratory study of veteran/rookie relations.* Unpublished master's thesis, University of Calgary, Calgary, Alberta.

Bryshun, J. and Young, K. (1999). "Sport related hazing," in P. White and K. Young (Eds.), *Sport and gender in Canada,* 269–289. Oxford University Press.

Davidson, L. (2001). "Qualitative research and making meaning from adventure: A case study of boys experiences of outdoor education at school," *Journal of adventure education and outdoor learning* 1: 11–21.

Daniels, W.R. (1994). *Breakthrough performance: Managing for speed and flexibility.* Act Publishing.

Eigen, L.D. (June 1994). *Alcohol practices, policies and potentials of American colleges and universities: An OSAP white paper.* MD: U.S. Department of Health and Human Services, Office for Substance Abuse Prevention. Reprinted in

Rethinking rites of passage: Substance abuse on America's campuses. Center on Addiction and Substance Abuse. Columbia University.

Hastie, P.A. (1995). An ecology of a secondary school outdoor adventure camp. *Journal of teaching in physical education* 15: 79–97.

Hattie, J.A., Marsh, H.W., Neill, J.T., and Richards, G.E. (1997). "Adventure education and Outward Bound: Out-of-class experiences that make a lasting difference," *Review of educational research* 67: 43–87.

Holman, M. (November 1997). *Hazing in sport.* Paper presented at the North American Society for the Sociology of Sport, Toronto, Canada.

Hoover, N.C. (1999). *National survey: Initiation rites and athletics for NCAA sports teams.* Available at: www.alfred.edu/news/html/hazing_study_99.html.

Hoover, N.C. and Pollard, N.J. (2000). *Initiation rites in American high schools: A national survey.* Available at: www.alfred.edu/news/html/hazing_study.html.

Johnson, J. (2002). "Are sisters doing it for themselves? An analysis of gender and the sport initiation ceremony," *Journal of Canadian woman studies/Les cahiers de la femme* 21(3).

Johnson, J. (2000). *Sport hazing experiences in the context of anti-hazing policies: The case of two Southern Ontario universities.* M.Sc. thesis, University of Toronto.

MacRae, S., Moore, C., Savage, G., Soehner, D. and Priest, S. (1998). "Changes in risk taking propensity resulting from a ropes course experience," in C. Loynes, (Ed.). *Outdoor management development,* 50–54. Penrith, Cumbria: Adventure Education.

Meyer, B.B. (2000). The ropes and challenge course: A quasi-experimental examination. *Perceptual and Motor Skills* 90: 1249–1257.

_____. (1998). "The long-term effects of ropes course participation on a high school tennis team," *Journal of sport and exercise psychology* 20: S63.

Messner, M.A. and Sabo, D. (1994). *Sex, violence & power in sports: Rethinking masculinity.* Freedom, Cailfornia: Crossing Press.

Miller, P.S. (2000, October). *Offering adventure based activities as an alternative to initiation and hazing in sport.* Paper presented at the 15th Annual Association for the Advancement of Applied Sport Psychology. Conference, Nashville, Tennessee.

Neill, J.T. and Heubeck, B. (July, 1998). "Adolescent coping styles and outdoor education: Searching for the mechanisms of change," in *Exploring the boundaries of adventure therapy: International perspectives.* Proceedings of the International Adventure Therapy Conference, Australia.

Nuwer, H. (1999). *Wrongs of passage: Fraternities, sororities, hazing, and binge drinking.* Bloomington, IN: Indiana University Press.

Priest, S. and Lesperance, M.A. (1994). "Time series trend analysis in corporate team development." *Journal of experiential education* 17: 34–39.

Riordan, B.G. and Dane, R.Q. (1998). "Greek letter organizations and alcohol: Problems, policies, and programs," *New directions for student services* 81: 49–59.

Robinson, L. (1998). *Crossing the line: Violence and sexual assault in Canada's national sport*. Toronto: McClelland and Stewart.

List of Contributing Authors

Elizabeth J. Allan, PhD, is Assistant Professor in the College of Education and Human Development at the University of Maine, where she teaches courses for the Masters and Doctoral degree programs in Educational Leadership. Dr. Allan has been involved in educating about hazing since the early 1990s, when she proposed and coordinated lobbying efforts for the passage of a state-wide anti-hazing law in New Hampshire. She has written a number of essays, book chapters, and encyclopedia entries on the topic of hazing, and is the co-founder and manager of www.stophazing.org, an educational website about hazing.

Cristina Caperchione is a graduate of the Faculty of Human Kinetics at the University of Windsor, Ontario, where she completed her Honours Bachelor of Human Kinetics and Masters of Human Kinetics. Her thesis examined the gender differences of coaches in their perceptions of hazing, leading to her work for this book. Currently, Cristina is completing her PhD at Central Queensland University, Australia.

R. Brian Crow is currently in his second year as Assistant Professor of Sport Management in the Department of Physical Education and Sport Management at Slippery Rock University. Dr. Crow is co-author of *Profiles of sport industry professionals: The people who make the games happen.* He is also the author of a chapter on hazing in athletics in the text *Law for sport and recreation managers.*

Gennaro DeAngelis is a former collegiate football player and coach. He earned a BSc in Psychology from Springfield College in 1999 and an MEd in Student Development in Higher Education from the University of Maine in 2003. His research interests include socially constructed masculinity, hazing behaviours, as well as student development and racial/ethnic identity formation theories.

Peter Donnelly, PhD, is Professor in the Faculty of Physical and Health Education at the University of Toronto. His areas of expertise include social aspects of sport and leisure, sport and leisure sub-cultures, politics of sport and leisure, and cultural studies and popular culture.

Margery Holman, PhD, is Associate Professor in the Faculty of Human Kinetics at the University of Windsor. Dr. Holman has been involved in sport professionally for over thirty years. Her teaching has included various sport-related courses, such as Principles of Coaching, Coaching Theory, Ethics in Sport and Physical Activity, Sport and the Law, and Gender Issues in Physical Activity. She continues to teach and research in these areas while maintaining connections with the sport community as a volunteer coach in a local high school, and in the design and administration of pro-grams for the development of females as sport participants and leaders. Dr. Holman has been the recipient of many awards over the course of her career, including City of Windsor Woman of the Year, and the University of Windsor's President's Employment Equity Award.

Jay Johnson is a PhD candidate at the University of Toronto. A lecturer at York University and the University of Waterloo, he is also affiliated with the LaMarsh Centre for the Study of Violence and Conflict Resolution.

Helen Jefferson Lenskyj is a professor at the Ontario Institute for Studies in Education, University of Toronto. As a sport sociologist, Dr. Lenskyj has specialized in gender and sexuality issues since 1980, and in Olympic industry critiques since 1992. Recent publications include *Out on the field: Gender, sport and sexuality* (Women's Press, 2003), *The best Olympics ever? Social impacts of Sydney 2000* (SUNY, 2002), and *Inside the Olympic industry: Power, politics and activism* (SUNY, 2000). Her expertise lends itself well to the critique of hazing in sport.

Greg Malszecki is on faculty at York University's School of Kinesiology and Health Science, and is also a member of the board for the LaMarsh Centre on Research on Violence and Conflict Resolution. Dr. Malszecki's work on the sociocultural studies of sport investigates the links between war, gender, and sport. His scholarship is aimed at connecting forms of violence into a coherent theory of violence rooted in the gender order instead of in "human nature." This work provides the foundation by which he has presented hazing in the military as a source for understanding hazing in sport.

Patricia Miller received a BA in Psychology from McGill University in 1993, an MA in Sport Psychology from the University of Ottawa in 1996, and a PhD in Sport Psychology from the Faculty of Physical Education and Health at the University of Toronto in 2001. Dr. Miller currently teaches at the university level, where she also researches issues related to the psychosocial development of high-level athletes. In addition, Trish works as a sport psychology consultant with coaches and athletes at the high school, university, and national level.

Hank Nuwer is an Indiana journalist and journalism professor at Franklin College and at the Indiana University School of Journalism in Indianapolis. He is the author of three books on hazing, and is a past adviser to Alfred University on its NCAA survey of hazing among college athletes, referred to in a number of the chapters of this book. Hank is a leading expert in North America on the topic of hazing.

Dennis R. Phillips has been a college professor and administrator for twenty-two years, the past eleven at the University of Southern Mississippi. He is currently the Graduate Coordinator for the School of Human Performance and Recreation at USM. Dr. Phillips has also been a college athlete and coach. He has taken an active role in education and policy on the issue of hazing in athletic settings. His writings include a chapter on hazing in athletics in *Law for sport and recreation managers* and co-authorship of the book *Profiles of sport industry professionals: The people who make the games happen.*

Laura Robinson is a former national-level athlete in Nordic skiing and cycling. She has been a sportswriter since 1990. Her book, *Crossing the line: Violence and sexual assault in Canada's national sport*, challenged the roots of Canadian hockey when it was published in 1998. She has won national and international awards for her investigative journalism in sport.

Brian Trota holds a BA in both English and History from York University. Brian is a host and a producer of GameOn, a weekly sports show on CHRY 105.5 FM, along with Jatinder Dhoot and Jon Levett. In his studies, Brian has explored the history of hazing. He shared this interest with his radio audience by recently hosting a show on the topic.